MYSTERY, HISTORY, & TRUTH

Susan Blumenthal

Schiffer
Publishing Ltd.

4880 Lower Valley Road, Atglen, Pennsylvania 19310

Santa Fe Architecture © *John Tomaselli. Image from BigStockPhotos.com.*

All photos by the author unless otherwise noted.

Other Schiffer Books on Related Subjects:

Santa Fe & Taos: A History in Postcards, 0-7643-2384-9, $24.95

A Journey through Northern Arizona, 978-0-7643-3010-0, $24.99

Scare-Izona: A Guide to Arizona's Legendary Haunts, 978-0-7643-2844-2, $14.95

Spirits of Dallas, 978-0-7643-3036-0, $14.99

Schiffer Books are available at special discounts for bulk purchases for sales promotions or premiums. Special editions, including personalized covers, corporate imprints, and excerpts can be created in large quantities for special needs. For more information contact the publisher:

Published by Schiffer Publishing Ltd.
4880 Lower Valley Road
Atglen, PA 19310
Phone: (610) 593-1777; Fax: (610) 593-2002
E-mail: Info@schifferbooks.com

For the largest selection of fine reference books on this and related subjects, please visit our web site at: **www.schifferbooks.com**. We are always looking for people to write books on new and related subjects. If you have an idea for a book please contact us at the above address.

This book may be purchased from the publisher. Include $5.00 for shipping.
Please try your bookstore first. You may write for a free catalog.

In Europe, Schiffer books are distributed by
Bushwood Books
6 Marksbury Ave.
Kew Gardens
Surrey TW9 4JF England
Phone: 44 (0) 20 8392-8585; Fax: 44 (0) 20 8392-9876
E-mail: info@bushwoodbooks.co.uk
Website: www.bushwoodbooks.co.uk
Free postage in the U.K., Europe; air mail at cost.

Copyright © 2009 by Susan Blumenthal
Library of Congress Control Number: 2008937071

Designed by Stephanie Daugherty
Type set in GrekoDeco/NewsGoth BT
ISBN: 978-0-7643-3175-6
Printed in the United States of America

ACKNOWLEDGEMENTS

I wish to express my most sincere gratitude to all the people who so generously shared with me their stories of Santa Fe ghosts and the stories behind the stories. In particular I would like to thank Raymond and Betty Kirsting for sharing their wonderful old family photographs and telling me the "real" story about the house at 122 Grant Avenue...before it became haunted, and Robert Ach, who shared his family history, shedding new light on the engimatic Julia Staab.

Others who shared their remarkable experiences, knowledge, or expertise include Artie Garcia, Brother Lester Lewis, Cody Polston and the Southwest Ghost Hunters Association, Steve Hererra, Richard Lindsley, Vanessa Schultz, Suzanne Alba, Adelaido (Lalo) Ortega, Connie Hernandez, Laura Holt, Jackie Pacheco, Isabelle Koomoa, Sabra and LaDonna, Jean Shaumberg, Stefanie Beninato, Hugh Horan, Kelly McCarthy, David Salazar, Debby Montoya, Gloria Castillo, Tobi Ives, Lisa Vertelli, and Bernadine Santistevan.

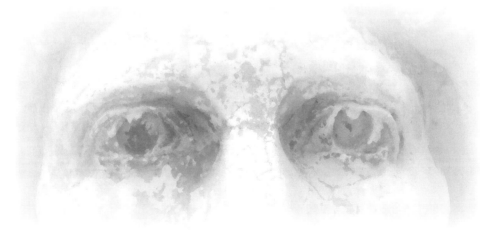

CONTENTS

AN INTRODUCTION TO GHOSTS 6

    To Believe or Not Believe.. 6

    A Dead Mother's Goodbye.. 11

    A Ghost Named Earl.. 17

CHAPTER ONE: La Fonda..23

CHAPTER TWO: The Grant Avenue House...............................31

CHAPTER THREE: The Playful Child Ghost...........................54

CHAPTER FOUR: San Miguel Mission 60

CHAPTER FIVE: The Oldest House...............................80

CHAPTER SIX: La Posada & the Mysterious Julia Staab 94

CHAPTER SEVEN: The Loretto Chapel...................................115

CHAPTER EIGHT: Palace of the Governors 128

CHAPTER NINE: Hotel St. Francis 131

CHAPTER TEN: Casa Real and La Residencia.......................136

CHAPTER ELEVEN: El Delirio & the School

    of American Research...143

CHAPTER TWELVE: Santa Fe Indian School..........................160

CHAPTER THIRTEEN: Restaurant Ghosts...........................166

    Analco Barrio 166

        Upper Crust Pizza • The Pink Adobe • The Guadalupe Café

    Canyon Road... 175

        Geronimo • El Farol

CHAPTER FOURTEEN: Profile of a Ghost Hunter....................182

    Orbs & Other Photographic Phenomenon 188

CHAPTER FIFTEEN: The New Mexico State Prison................192

CHAPTER SIXTEEN: La Llorona...211

CHAPTER SEVENTEEN: The Driving "Ghost"...........................217

BIBLIOGRAPHY 219

INDEX...222

AN INTRODUCTION TO GHOSTS

TO BELIEVE OR NOT BELIEVE

S anta Fe proudly calls itself "The City Different," and New Mexico is dubbed "The Land of Enchantment." It's no surprise then that stories of the supernatural are as abundant as sunshine in Santa Fe. One of the oldest cities in the United States, Santa Fe played a prominent role in the Spanish colonization, the Wild West era, and, in contemporary times, the development of the atomic bomb. Santa Fe is renown for its art galleries—it's the third largest art market in the United States behind New York and Los Angeles; world-renowned opera; five-star lodging and dining; fiery local cuisine; fascinating history... and *its* ghosts.

If the twisting, intertwining ladder pillars of Santa Fe's DNA are long, vibrant histories and unique, colorful legends, then ghost stories, paranormal anomalies, supernatural experiences, and unique spiritual perspectives are the mysterious rungs that connect them.

From a headless horseman said to ride down Alto Street along the Santa Fe River, brandishing a sword, to the oft-repeated stories of restless spirits at several of the city's finest hotels, to houses haunted by aggressive ghosts, to dark stories of strange occurrences related to hangings, gun battles, and the most bloody and infamous prison riot in U.S. history, Santa Fe boasts a dense and diverse ghost population. Some of the ghosts have attained celebrity status and are more famous in death than their physical bodies were in life. Their stories are so fascinating, their manifestations so intriguing...that Santa Fe, with a population of less than 100,000 people, supports four highly competitive ghost tour companies with more always attempting to break into the market.

The City Different is so steeped in ghost lore that in June of 2007 local news stations all over New Mexico broadcast surveillance camera video from the Judicial Complex showing a glowing orb moving purposefully across the screen with matter-of-fact speculation that it was a new Santa Fe ghost. According to an article in the *Santa Fe New Mexican*, one deputy proclaimed, "I say it's a ghost." There was heated speculation of exactly who the ghost had been in its earthly life. An employee at the District Attorney's Office said she believed the image was of a spirit. "It's a little girl, and she can't find where she needs to be. Somebody disturbed her." A clerk in the same building said she thought it might have been a ghost upset by the construction of the city's new convention center across the street. She said her husband, a sheriff's deputy, used to work in the courthouse at night when the county's dispatch center was located there and he used to hear footsteps, doors opening and closing, and elevators going up and down. A deputy said he thought it might be the ghost of a convicted murderer who took nine people hostage at the courthouse twenty-five years prior and was shot and killed by a sheriff's deputy.

That's Santa Fe.

Because the city is so steeped in ghostly lore, and the unexplainable isn't uncommon, the first assumption—not the offbeat, last assumption—but the *FIRST* assumption, is that it's a ghost. The Courthouse Ghost video was posted on the web site "YouTube" and drew 75,000 hits in one week and even more speculation. Both ABC and CBS News picked up the story. Newspapers across the nation were quick to follow and the story spread internationally. It was Santa Fe after all, where the paranormal is considered normal, thus giving the Courthouse Ghost certain credibility just because of the city in which it was spotted.

Paranormal debunkers, eager to prove that it was really nothing, raced to the challenge and were able to produce a very brief re-creation of the event by putting an insect on the camera lens.

And that's part of the problem with ghosts. Many normal circumstances can appear supernatural and some supernatural events are so bizarre, so unbelievable that they are simply dismissed as impossible. Ghosts are controversial with a prevailing condescension: Either you "believe in" or "don't believe in" ghosts...much like children "believing in" the tooth fairy or Santa Claus. There's rarely a middle ground and believers and disbelievers are passionate about being right. Some insist that every bump in the night is a ghost and refuse to believe anything else while debunkers are unrelenting in their stance that there are no paranormal events and, usually with an air of intellectual superiority, there is *always* a "logical" explanation. They point eagerly to situations like the bug on the surveillance camera lens to make their point that paranormal events are always distortions of normal reality. Debunkers consider ghosts to be only fanciful folktales that some misguided adults *still* believe are real. Indeed, ghost and paranormal debunkers go to great lengths to "prove" ghosts and other paranormal events don't exist, as if to protect the poor naïve "believers" from their own ignorance. The debunkers' only reason for insisting ghosts aren't real is the tired, worn-out argument: no scientific proof.

But lack of scientific proof is hardly a reason to discount the existence of ghosts because what can be "proven" changes as technology advances. From microorganisms to sub-atomic particles, technology continues to reveal more information about mysterious, invisible worlds not accessible through our five senses. However, because of the likelihood of professional ridicule, don't expect that the brightest scientific minds are working on developing any devices for ghost hunting.

Dogs can interact with a complex, invisible world of scents, sometimes tracking them for miles and distinguishing one particular scent from potentially millions of other competing scents. Indeed, dogs are still the most reliable detectors of substances like explosives and drugs, yet scientists still only have vague ideas how they are able to track and identify scents with such accuracy. If dogs can interact with the invisible world of scents, why is it so difficult to believe that some people can detect and even interact with manifestations of energy?

Part of the ability to detect ghosts may have to do with something as simple as different levels of visual acuity and the actual anatomy and function of the human eye. One of the most common prologues to a ghost story or paranormal encounter begins, "I first caught something out of the corner of my eye." Interestingly, photoreceptor rod cells are concentrated at the outer edges of the retina. Rod cells, which are responsible for both peripheral and night vision, are extremely light sensitive and can detect a single photon of light. Rod cells are also densely packed and "wired" together so acuity is not precise but motion detection is, which is why peripheral vision images are not clearly defined. Rod cells are limited in the range of light spectrum they can detect and are most sensitive to the blue spectrum.

Whether it's an event that began with something caught in the corner of the eye, or other sensory experience, those who "believe" in ghosts, who have actually had a paranormal experience outside the boundaries of ordinary reality, will never be convinced that what happened was not "real." If some people are born with a gift for mathematics or excellent spelling, a high intellect, superb athletic skills, or any other talent, it should not be difficult to believe that some people are born with a greater sense of perception of things not of this visible reality. In most cases the people who have paranormal experiences don't seek them...*they* just happen. There are commonalities in an initial paranormal experience. First is denial, sometimes followed by fear, and then acceptance. Paranormal experiences and ghostly encounters can be very isolating because sharing them invites ridicule and suspicion of mental illness. As a result of this reverse superstition – that intelligent, rational people don't believe in ghosts – it's likely that paranormal encounters are actually quite common because the vast majority probably go unreported.

I know ghosts, spirits, residual human energy – whatever you want to call it – are real. I've had encounters and, as the experiences unfolded, my first response was extreme denial. However, at some point all you can do is surrender to the experience rather than talk yourself out of it. Because of my experiences I wanted to dig a little deeper into the ghost stories of Santa Fe and find the more personal side of the stories. I believe that stories and legends emerge from a profound seed of truth. And, just as a plant emerges from a seed and pushes its way to the light and grows and changes and no longer resembles the seed, so too does a good story grow. Perhaps that is what makes ghost stories such an easy target for debunkers—like the plant that no longer resembles the seed, an oft-told story may no longer resemble the seed truth of its source. Most ghost stories grew from the common elements of experiences like tragedy and trauma and loving attachment to a specific place or person. Those two themes are played out repeatedly in stories of ghostly encounters.

Indeed, those are the common elements of two of my stories. The first story, "A Dead Mother's Goodbye," happened to me when I was in my late twenties. It so confounded me that it was years before I told anybody about it. It also troubled me deeply and the only way I could deal with it at the time was to write about it extensively in my journal, which is why I can recall it in such precise detail this many years later. In a way, that experience cracked apart my closed attitude, so I learned to be more open and less skeptical, to acknowledge at least on a very personal level that I was more perceptive to things not of the material world. I had some strange experiences in childhood seeing things other people didn't see and was soundly ridiculed, so I developed a sort of heightened level of "rationality" and skepticism as a teenager and a show-me-the-proof defensiveness as a young adult. After all, who wants to be considered crazy? Now, I feel sadness for people who are like I used to be: those who cannot acknowledge that there just might be some things that are not explainable in the framework of ordinary reality as we know it.

There is so much more out there than just what meets the eye.

A Dead Mother's Goodbye

I was twenty-eight years old, a recently divorced mother with two toddlers, living in a rural area south of Albuquerque, New Mexico called Pajarito. It was February of 1978 and I was coming home from work with cranky children fussing in their car seats. Even with the pandemonium in the back seat I felt a sudden surge of anxiety as I turned onto the small dead-end road that led to my house. I was overwhelmed with a strange sense that something was terribly wrong. As I got out of the car to open the gate to my property, I noticed the small boy who had just moved in across the street standing in the doorway of the house with the door wide open to the late winter chill. A car was in front of the house with the driver's door open.

The house was a rental that I managed. I had rented it the previous summer to a physician who told me he would be doing a family practice residency at the University of New Mexico Hospital. Chuck was a personable fellow and very proud of his Native American heritage as a member of the Winnebago tribe. When he rented the house, he explained that his family would be joining him in several months, that his wife had prematurely delivered a son after he accepted the residency position. She was a Shoshone and staying with her family in Wyoming until the baby was strong enough to leave the hospital and travel.

Months passed and Chuck reported in passing that the baby was getting stronger, his work was going well, and he was learning more about the Native Americans of the Southwest through pow-wows and various organizations associated with the university.

Chuck's wife and children finally joined him in late January. He couldn't wait to introduce me to his wife Jennie and show off his three children; six-year old Eric, eighteen month-old Rita, and the tiny, tiny baby they named Courage.

As I drove my car in the driveway, I heard something very uncharacteristic for that rural farming area: sirens. When I got out to close the gate, a rescue squad truck with flashing lights slid around the corner of the dirt road, quickly followed by sheriff's cars and what looked like the entire Pajarito volunteer firefighting department in a variety of old pick-up trucks. The rescue van skidded to a stop in front of the house across the street. Rescue workers scrambled out, shouting and mobilizing gear. My children, terrified, began screaming and I hustled them into the house and set them down with toys. I went out to the gate and watched the frantic activity. The air crackled with garbled radio communications. When I spotted one of the volunteer firefighters who didn't seem to be engaged in the activity, I went over to him and asked him what was happening.

"Heart attack. The kid found her unconscious on the floor when he came home from school. Called the dad. He called us," the man said bluntly.

Heart attack, I thought, incredulous. I knew Jennie was only thirty years old. As I pondered this seemingly incomprehensible situation of a six-year-old boy finding his mother, the firefighter added, "If you know the guy, are any kind of a friend or anything, you should go to him because he's a wreck and could use some comfort." He gestured at an hysterical Chuck, who was being led out of the house by a sheriff's deputy.

"Yes, of course." I said, not having any idea how I could be of any comfort in such a tragic situation.

As I walked up to Chuck, he embraced me like a drowning man grabbing a life preserver. He began weeping in anguish, incoherently trying to explain: "She had a congenital heart condition. We thought she was fine. Medication. Maybe the two little ones so close together was too much. Eric found her. Don't know how long she was … I froze. I couldn't help. I'm a doctor and I couldn't help!"

Over the din I heard a child crying in the house.

"Let me take care of your children," I said calmly. "You do what you need to do."

We went inside. I hurried past the kitchen, not looking, not wanting to see, but hearing a paramedic shouting into his radio, "No pupil response. Flat EKG." Then, "Clear!"

Chuck wailed.

I went to the bedroom where I heard the child crying. Six year-old Eric was huddled in a corner. It was eighteen-month-old Rita crying. Baby Courage slept in his crib, oblivious. Eric wanted to know what happened to his mom. I felt suffocated by the fear of dealing with the situation, of making a mistake, saying something wrong that would only increase the children's emotional trauma. I picked up Rita and cuddled and cooed to her until she stopped crying. I told Eric that there were lots of people trying to help his mother and that the best thing we could do was to stay out of their way.

An ashen-faced Chuck came into the bedroom, and I could see the gurney being quickly wheeled past the door with some sort of bag apparatus, IV pole, and white-sheeted figure. "Go, go with her," I told Chuck. "I'll take good care of the kids."

"Bottles and formula in the kitchen…diapers are…diapers are…."

"Just go," I said. "Don't worry about this. I'll find what I need."

Chuck ran out of the room and minutes later the sirens wailed.

"Okay," I said to Eric, trying to sound cheerful. "You get to spend the night at my house. You can play with my son. He's almost four." Oh, no, I thought: My kids. They're alone. Another wave of panic washed over me as I imagined something horrible happening to my children while they were alone and unattended.

I told Eric I'd be right back and went around the corner to the tiny kitchen to look for bottles and formula. I gasped at the scene of an innocent moment suddenly, incomprehensibly, interrupted by tragedy: Soapy water in the sink... Yellow dish gloves, one hanging off the edge of the sink, one on the floor... Broken and twisted eyeglasses on the floor... A few small spots of blood... And the feeling, I knew instinctively, was death. I was so overwhelmed with emotion, grief, and horror that I nearly fainted. Nausea churned in my stomach, making its way to my throat. I was terrified of death. I had a phobia about it. Growing up, I was told that I'd broken my grandfather's heart because I didn't attend my grandmother's funeral. I was simply too terrified. And here I was confronted with my absolute worst fear.

Somebody had died here.

I quickly gathered baby bottles that Jenny had just washed from the dish drainer, rummaged in the cupboards until I found formula, and headed to the bathroom for the diapers. I quickly loaded everything into the diaper bag that Eric held out to me mutely. I scooped up the baby, hoisted little Rita up on to my hip with the other hand, and we headed across the street to my house.

Not even the confusion and chaos of trying to care for five children under the age of six could distract me from thinking about the tragedy I had just witnessed, from the feeling of death that had created this vacuum of fear and dread that seemed to swallow up all rational thought.

Time moved in slow motion as I tried to get the children ready for bed, as I tried to deflect Eric's questions about his mother. Finally, I got all the children but Rita settled and asleep. Somehow, she seemed to be the most disturbed. She was crying and fussy and had no language to express what I knew must be a terrible fear or sense of loss. I sat down with her in the antique rocking chair that I had spent so many hours rocking my own babies and began rocking her and singing to her and talking to her. As with my own children, when they were particularly cranky and I was feeling impatient or keyed up, I attempted to first create calmness in myself by imagining how many other mothers had rocked their babies in this beautiful old chair I'd found in a West Virginia barn and painstakingly refinished. The rhythmic creak, creak, creak seemed to have just as much a calming effect on me as it did on babies.

Suddenly, I felt a presence. A very commanding presence. All the tiny hairs rose up on my body and a chill washed over me, a deep, penetrating chill. I couldn't see anything, but much as I tried to fight against the very I idea, I knew. I knew with absolute certainty that Jenny was there in the room with me. I was terrified. My heart pounded. I was shaking. I tried to talk myself out of the feeling, tried to tell myself it was just anxiety, that there was nothing there. It was impossible for her to be there. Impossible. I focused on rocking, rocking faster, head down over the baby as I whispered to her and started to sing to her. But the spirit demanded my attention with an energy of astonishing force, demanded I acknowledge her presence.

I looked up, and while I couldn't see anything, I could certainly feel something, a powerful energy. Involuntarily, I kissed the baby's cheek and cuddled her closer. Tears suddenly poured down my face. The spirit told me, "Thank you." And at that moment my fear was transformed to peace and excruciating sorrow. I knew she had come back to say goodbye. "Thank you for caring for them," she told me. It wasn't that I heard the words audibly so much as I felt them powerfully pressed into my soul, into the deepest part of my consciousness. There was absolutely no mistaking or misinterpreting the message.

Out loud I said, "It's what I would have wanted somebody to do for mine." It was all I could manage to communicate. It was soul-to-soul, but more, it was mother-to-mother. She lingered briefly and then...she was gone.

Rita fell asleep and I carefully laid her down on a mat next to Eric in my son's room. Late in the evening, as I was sitting in stunned silence trying to understand what had happened, I was jolted by the phone ringing. It was Chuck with the news I already knew. Sobbing, he told me they'd been able to revive Jenny in the ambulance and keep her alive on life support in the hospital, but since there was no indication of brain activity, he'd let them disconnect her and she had died. With a ragged sigh, he told me he was home and would come get the kids. I said, "No, they're fine. They're all sleeping peacefully. You don't need to worry about them right now."

There was a very long silence and then he said, "Well, if they stay with you, there is something I need you to do. A favor. Something important."

"Sure, anything."

"Please put a small knife next to their beds. You can tuck it under a mattress."

"Umm, ok." I started to question it, but then I realized it must be a custom of his people.

"And, something else I must ask."

"Sure."

"Turn them so they are not facing east, so that their heads are not toward the east. And, please..." there was a long pause as if it was very difficult for him to say, as if he feared ridicule, "cover all your windows tightly so that light can't shine out."

"Ok. I'll do that," I said, trying to sound as matter-of-fact as possible.

He took a deep breath and paused before he tried to explain, "Her spirit might come back...to try to take the children."

Everything in me wanted to tell him she had just been there. That she didn't try to take her children, that she just wanted to say goodbye…and to thank me. Tears burned in my eyes. I just couldn't tell him. Even though he could share his belief in the spirit world, ask me to perform what might be his people's sacred death ritual, and by doing that invite condemnation and ridicule, which he had surely experienced with white culture, I could not share with him, could not tell him his wife's spirit had blessed their children with a goodbye and that Rita had calmed down. Sadly, I was afraid of sounding weird or that he might not believe me.

After we hung up, I gently tried to rearrange the children without waking them so that their heads were not to the east. I tucked small paring knives next to them, agonizing over whether they would be adequate, if they would be considered "real" knives because steak knives seemed too dangerous around small children. Next, I began gathering up old sheets and towels to tightly cover the windows. I heard a strong cadence of drumbeats and then chanting. As I went to cover my large kitchen window with a sheet, I saw a bonfire in the pasture next to Chuck's house. I couldn't pick Chuck out of the dark circle of figures, their arms intertwined, as they raised their haunting chant louder with the cadence of the drum, but I knew his must be the most agonized of the voices.

A Ghost Named Earl

I had to sell the house in Pajarito later in 1978 as part of my divorce settlement. In those times a single woman buying a house was rare and my options were limited. I was fortunate to find a real estate dream: a run down house in an area of much more expensive homes in another rural area, the North Valley. I knew from simply looking at it from the outside—even though it was in terrible shape—it was my house. It was a for-sale-by-owner and, because of the desirable location, when I made it to a pay phone I was told there were already two bids on it. Through a strange series of events, my bid was accepted and I bought it without ever going inside.

It had been a rental house for more than ten years with numerous tenants. As I explored it for the first time, I discovered many long-neglected features of the house that were very obviously constructed with great care and attention to detail: An intricate gazebo complete with brick barbeque grill nearly invisible in a tangle of overgrown vines; a small pond filled with debris; and, inside, I could see that the garage had been converted into what was once called a "den" with heavy pine paneling, Mexican tile bar, and brick fireplace. The yard was a mess of weeds taller than the top of my head, but there was a venerable old cottonwood tree that shaded the entire back of the house.

As I began working on the house I sometimes felt like I had extra strength, as if somebody was helping me move heavy things. Since I didn't have a wheelbarrow, I used my children's red wagon with a barrel in it to haul trash. It seemed to zip along effortlessly no matter how much I loaded it up. As the months passed, I began to sense a presence…a presence that was very pleased that my children and I had moved in. Indeed, my daughter who was about two and a half at the time seemed to strike up a great friendship with this presence. There was a short hallway between two bedrooms. My children shared the larger bedroom and the smaller I used as an office. In the middle of this hallway was a full-length mirror and an old-fashioned floor furnace. My daughter would get out of bed, walk in her sleep, and stand in front of the mirror on the furnace grate. Then, she would talk to the presence that I named—for no particular reason—Earl. She had vague recollections of talking to a man, but no specific memory of the event, when I would ask her about it the next day. It was very creepy at first, but then it just became commonplace. Several years later when the movie "Poltergeist" came out. I joked about how Steven Spielberg simply changed the mirror to a television that the child used to communicate with the ghosts.

Sometimes Earl was mischievous. Things would turn up missing. Something set in one place would inexplicably turn up in another. For the most part Earl seemed very pleased that I was fixing up a house he loved. For the most part...

After living in the house for about five years I decided to gut the kitchen and have a friend who was a skilled finish carpenter install pre-made cabinets ordered from a local hardware store. I'd never told anyone about Earl. He was my crazy aunt in the attic of whom I never spoke. After all, stating there is ghost in your house sets you up for cheap jokes and ridicule. I felt oddly nervous about tearing out things and making such a major modification to the house. Still, the kitchen really needed updating.

At one point in the demolition process, as my friend took a pry bar to a piece of intricately cut trim, he said, "Wow, I get the distinct feeling that somebody didn't like that."

And, even though the hardware store representative had seemed to meticulously measure for the cabinets, when they arrived, not a single one fit. They were all off by anything from a few inches to more than six. At first I assumed incompetence on the part of the hardware store representative, but then I wondered if Earl had a hand in the inaccuracy. It was months before new cabinets could be manufactured, which forced us to live in the chaos of a gutted kitchen with no means to cook anything except in the microwave precariously perched on top of the refrigerator. Sometimes it was as if I could feel Earl gloating over my exasperation at the situation.

I remarried, but our relationship had some rocky times. One night Earl made it very clear he did not like conflict. It was about 2 a.m. and my husband and I were embroiled in a bitter argument, screaming and yelling at each other. We were standing at one end of the "den" room that I had converted to a bedroom. Suddenly, the ceiling over our heads that had recently suffered some slight damage from a small roof leak burst open, showering us with not only a cascade of plaster and wood, but also small, empty whiskey bottles. Picking bits of plaster out of our hair, my husband and I stared at each other incredulous. The ceiling right above us—not two feet away where there was actually more signs of water leakage—but *directly* above us had actually burst open. We were both dumbfounded. My husband got up on a stepladder and peered in the hole with a flashlight while I started cleaning up the debris.

"Looks like ol' Earl was a bit of a drinker. The whole ceiling is filled with bottles for as far as I can see. Miniatures. Pints. No big bottles though," my husband said.

After living in the house for more than eighteen years, I put it on the market to sell when we began construction of a new house on a remarkable piece of land that my father had bought in the 1950s.

Earl was not pleased.

After eighteen years of home improvement projects, the house had gone from the neighborhood dump to the finest house on the street. Great curb and show appeal in what had become an extremely desirable area with skyrocketing real estate prices. Strangely, prospective buyers would come in, admire, and then quickly head for the door.

I stashed everything in the house except the bare essentials in a storage locker so it would "show" better and appear less cluttered. The realtor hustled, holding more frequent open houses. I baked brownies for the open houses and made sure that the oven was warming a mélange of orange peels, cinnamon, and vanilla in a bowl of water.

The realtor was completely flummoxed. Nobody was interested.

After months of this I began pleading with Earl. When that didn't work I took to screaming at him. After the whiskey bottle incident, I got the distinct feeling that Earl was in an unhappy marriage with a shrewish wife who yelled a lot. The "den" had been his refuge and he had created some sort of a hole in a closet to stuff the empty bottles in until they filled the ceiling. I threatened to hunt him down in the afterlife and be another version of his wife if he didn't quit shooing people out of the house.

I bought a St. Joseph real estate kit at a religious articles store and, even though it seemed very disrespectful, I followed the directions and buried the poor little plastic saint upside down.

I talked sweetly to Earl.

I smudged the house with so much sage I was afraid it smelled like an Amsterdam hashish den.

Still, no success.

When the new house was finished, we moved out. As it happened, both my older children—by then adults—were at transition points in their lives so they agreed to move into the house and pay rent. That would be a big help in managing two house payments.

When my daughter invited her new boyfriend over, as soon as he walked in the door, the first thing he said was, "I feel like I've been here before." It was a statement he would make on several subsequent visits.

After a brief "honeymoon" period my son and daughter began fighting over the types of things roommates fight over: houseguests, food ownership, and cleanliness. These conflicts must have convinced Earl that a new resident would be preferable to two bickering twenty-somethings and the house suddenly sold to a quiet single woman.

But the story of Earl wasn't over. Indeed, it would only get more bizarre.

My daughter married the boyfriend who had visited her at the house. Several years after they married my daughter's husband, who had been adopted as an infant, began a search to find his birth parents. With my daughter helping with the research, they eventually found his birth mother in Texas and traveled there to meet her. In the awkward getting-to-know each other introductions, the birth mother explained that she had gotten pregnant at sixteen and in "those days" such a thing was scandalous. Her mother kicked her out and she moved in with her grandparents while an aunt searched for a "home" to send her to out of state. She mentioned that her grandparents lived in the North Valley area outside of Albuquerque. My daughter, in an effort to find some common ground, said she grew up in the North Valley and they chatted about what a lovely place it was. The birth mother said that she had fond memories of the house on Charles Place. My daughter exclaimed, "I lived on Charles Place!"

The same house that had felt so familiar to her boyfriend was in fact the home of his birth mother's grandparents. And the ghost, "Earl" (whose real name was not Earl), turned out to be was the grandfather of her husband. The birth mother confirmed our family lore about "Earl." He was a kindly, hen-pecked man who dearly loved working on the house and was very attached to it. The grandmother could be rather shrewish.

These profound and personal experiences with ghosts helped me emptathize when people shared their stories and understand why some might want to keep their stories to themselves. It also inspired me to look for the "real" ghost stories and personal accounts behind the legends and lore. In doing so, I met some wonderful people and heard some amazing tales.

1

LA FONDA

La Fonda.

La Fonda is a Santa Fe landmark just off the Santa Fe Plaza. Like many buildings in Santa Fe it has been reincarnated many times, however, true to its name La Fonda (the inn) has always been a place of lodging, possibly as far back as Spanish colonial times. The Santa Fe Trail ended just off the plaza and, as it grew into a major trade and travel route, the La Fonda attracted an odd assortment of guests; mountain men and trappers. Even Captain William Becknell, who blazed the Santa Fe Trail, stayed there in 1821.

Perhaps as a nod to the political correctness of the day, the name was changed to the U.S. Hotel when New Mexico became a United States Territory in 1848 and the inn was purchased by Anglos. Like many such establishments in the Wild West era, the inn's gambling hall was a major destination, a wild raucous place, attracting military officers, cowboys, and professional gamblers.

The back of the hotel was the scene of a lynching in 1857. Ten years later a shouting match in the lobby resulted in a murder. When the Honorable John P. Slough, Chief Justice of the Territorial Supreme Court, called Captain Rynerson, a member of the Territorial Legislature representing Dona Ana County, a liar and a thief, Rynerson pulled his gun and shot Slough in the stomach. It was an incident curiously prophetic for New Mexico politics are bizarrely contentious to this day. As often happened in frontier justice, Rynerson was tried but later acquitted.

In the mid 1800s, the hotel was sold again and became The Exchange Hotel. It would operate under this name for nearly six decades. Also during this time, several tunnels leading to the courthouse were constructed underneath the hotel.

In 1922, on the site of the previous inns, the current version of the La Fonda was built. The Atchison, Topeka, and Santa Fe Railroad acquired La Fonda in 1925 and it became one of the legendary Harvey Houses. Renowned Southwest architects John Gaw Meem and Mary Coulter remodeled and redecorated the La Fonda using native rugs, pottery, and art. La Fonda became the favored destination of artists, movie stars, and politicians. The La Fonda was sold to its current owners in 1968.

Today, the La Fonda Hotel is still one of Santa Fe's premier hotels, but over the years it has acquired its share of ghosts. Like many Santa Fe ghost stories, particularly those related to lodging, the legends seem to bear identical wording that can be traced back to the New Mexico Department of Tourism website. The website lists these legends about La Fonda's ghosts:

• "Some people believe that the Honorable Judge Slough continues to walk its hallways. However, more often reported is the ghost of the distraught salesman who jumped into the well after losing all of his company's money. The hotel's dining room, called the La Plazuela, is situated directly over the old well and both guests and staff alike have reported the sight of a ghostly figure that walks to the center of the room, then seemingly jumps into the floor and disappears.

• "Other reported phenomena includes an apparition that haunts the Santa Fe Room, as well as a spirit that walks the hallways near the La Terraza, a restaurant located on the east side of the hotel's third floor.

• "In the 1970s, a guest reportedly called the front desk to complain that someone was walking up and down the hallway in front of his room. When an employee was sent to investigate, he saw a tall man in a long, black coat disappear into a stairwell. However, when he followed him to the stairs, there was no sign of the mysterious visitor."

The La Fonda is a gracious old hotel whose original Harvey House charm hasn't been "updated" away. La Plazuela, the Interior Courtyard restaurant, has an almost ethereal glow from a ceiling of frosted glass panels that diffuse and filter the light. The room, with its vivid turquoise trim, features brightly colored paintings on windows and glass panels and a host of ficus trees festooned with tiny sparkling lights. Hardly the sort of place one would expect to find "a ghostly figure that walks to the center of the room, then seemingly jumps into the floor and disappears."

The Southwest Ghost Hunters Association (SGHA) made three visits to La Fonda, in 1998, 2005, and 2007. They describe these thorough investigations in fascinating detail, complete with video of the 2007 visit, on its website. Their first investigation included the discovery of previously unknown doors in a basement area that no master keys fit. Speculation was that the doors led to old subterranean incarceration chambers for outlaws and Indians,

La Plazuela, the Interior Courtyard restaurant at La Fonda.

but perhaps they were the remains of the tunnels to the old courthouse from the previous version of La Fonda. Besides the stories reported by the State of New Mexico Tourism department, the Southwest Ghost Hunters record these fascinating stories on their website, some of which seem to elaborate other historical stories of the La Fonda.

> • "On June 14, 1862 a soldier named James Bennet visited the La Fonda and wrote in his journal about what he witnessed. Bennet was seated in La Fonda's lobby when a cowboy came in and started shooting up the hotel. The cowboy said he was from Texas and was getting even for a friend of his who was killed. The cowboy shot a lawyer in the stomach and another man in the arm before he was captured and thrown into jail. Later that night the cowboy from Texas was lynched and hung in the backyard of the La Fonda.
>
> • The hotel is also home to an apparition of a young bride who was murdered on her wedding night by an ex-lover. She mainly haunts

the wedding suite (Room 510). A night auditor of twenty years has witnessed the apparition of a bride walking into the hotel lobby, only to vanish as she approaches the front desk. The same apparition has also been seen on the elevator, in the hallway outside room 510, and in the basement.

• One evening, a security guard was making his rounds of the hotel when he entered one of the hotel's banquet rooms called the New Mexico Room. The room appeared to be empty. When he was halfway across the floor he 'felt' someone and sensed that someone was behind him. Turning around, he saw a man in the middle of the floor moving towards the center of the room. When he confronted the man, the figure *disappeared* through the floor. Freaked out by the man's sudden disappearance, he ran to the front desk. Just as he arrived, the manager came running down the hall in a state of near panic. The manager said that he was downstairs in housekeeping and he 'felt' an icy cold presence move through him. The area the manager was in is directly underneath the New Mexico Room, where the figure disappeared through the floor.

• Two different ghosts haunt the hotel's bar. The first ghost is that of a "cowboy"—he is often seen sitting at the bar around 2 to 3 a.m. When approached, the figure disappears. The second ghost is an African-American gentleman who may be one of the former bartenders. A workman who was working on the tile in the bell tower saw this ghost and he claims there is no way the man could have entered the area without being seen as there was only one door and he was blocking it.

Other miscellaneous events include:

• Room 274 (at the front of the hotel) — Housekeeping was going to clean up room when she witnessed someone lying in the bed with the sheets pulled up over his head. Thinking that he had not checked out yet, she returned to the front desk, double checked, and found out the room was supposed to be vacant. She got the houseman to go with her to wake up the man and get him out of the room. The houseman went to the form on the bed, pulled back covers, and there was no one there.

• Elevator to the bell tower – Security guards making rounds would always be met by the elevator...even on empty floors. Heading down the stairs, he would still be met by the elevator.

A guest using the elevator to get to his room saw a shadow that did not match his own shadow. This typically happens only with the left elevator.

• The fireplace in the Santa Fe room apparently lights itself in the winter if wood is placed in it.

A security guard doing paperwork near the fireplace sat down, left the area for a moment, came back, and the furniture was rearranged.

• Auditory phenomena reported near food/liquor storage areas supposedly happens more often to new employees.

Because these La Fonda stories frequently involved employees, I expected everyone at the La Fonda would be familiar with them. However that was not the case when I visited. The girls at the front desk giggled when I asked them about ghosts and directed me to the concierge. The concierge laughs and tells me that there is a man—Lalo—who has worked at the hotel "forever." "And I mean forever," he adds for emphasis. Because I discovered that some Santa Fe properties and even some ghost tours consider "their" ghosts to be "proprietary," I ask the concierge to direct me to the hotel manager. La Fonda's manager, Lisa Vertelli, says that's she's heard some vague stories about ghosts, but encourages me to find bellman Lalo Ortega, an employee who had been with the hotel more than fifty years. "If anybody knows the stories or has had any first-hand experiences, it's going to be Lalo," she said with a laugh.

Again, not exactly what I expected when there are so many stories of sightings and the La Fonda is always a destination on ghost tours.

I make my way to Mr. Ortega's office off the La Fonda's underground parking garage—apparently the site of some Native

American burials since construction had to be halted and remains investigated and identified by archeologist before construction could proceed a number of years ago. Mr. Ortega's office is a long, windowless room filled with chairs, luggage, and miscellaneous boxes. He pulls a banquet room type chair off a stack and urges me to sit down. He is a small, lively silver-haired man dressed in dark pants, white shirt, and sporting a cast pewter silver bolo tie with the deeply etched words "La Fonda." I tell him that the concierge told me that he had worked at La Fonda "forever" and he laughs, "Well, I don't know about forever, but it's a long time."

He tells me that he started at La Fonda in 1943 as a room service waiter. Then he went off to war. He resumed working at the La Fonda again in 1950 when he got out of the service. In all this time working at the La Fonda, he had one remarkable, bizarre experience.

"Very late one night," he begins, "a guest up on the fourth floor called down to the front desk and said that somebody was walking back and forth in front their room. I decided if it was somebody up to no good, I should go up the backstairs to the fourth floor to maybe sneak up on them. When I got there I saw a man standing in the hallway. He had on a very long black coat and a tall, uh, what do you call it? An Abe Lincoln hat?"

"A stove pipe hat?" I offer.

"Yes, a stove pipe hat. A tall black stove pipe hat. When I tried to get a better look at him, he turned so I couldn't see his face." Mr. Ortega jerks sideways in his chair to demonstrate. "And then he took off toward the stairs. I followed him. He ran down the stairs and I tried to keep up, but all I could see was the bottom of his coat every time he went around a landing. He went all the way to the basement. When he got to the basement...he just disappeared."

I recognize that story as the one of an employee chasing the tall man in the long coat in the early 1970s from the New Mexico Tourism Department website.

I ask Mr. Ortega when that incident happened.

"Hmmm. I think it was in the early fifties, that was back when we had bellmen on duty around the clock."

Because there are so many other stories, I was sure that Mr. Ortega must have at least heard them. "What about the other stories of ghosts?" I ask.

"Well, the only thing I've heard is that they used to hang people in the lobby."

"There's supposed to be a ghost that disappears in the floor of La Plazuela. The story is that it's a salesman who gambled away all his company's money and jumped from the balcony into the well in the center of the courtyard."

"Jumped into the well, ehh?" Mr. Ortega asks. "I do know one story like that."

"Great! What happened?" I say, quickly turning the page in my notebook, excited that I'm going to be getting a unique twist on an old tale.

"There was this front desk manager," he begins, waiting to make sure I'm writing. "He was going to show this couple the spa." Mr. Ortega watches me write and when I look up he smiles. "He walks up to the spa. And then..." he pauses for dramatic effect while I scribble furiously to keep up, "he falls in."

Mr. Ortega laughs loudly and slaps his thigh. And I laugh with him. It's a good joke. He explains that the only story he can tell is the one that happened to him and that he really doesn't know about any other stories, but adds, "So much has happened here."

I thank him for his time, and smile as I leave thinking, "And then...he falls in."

THE
GRANT AVENUE HOUSE

Grant Avenue House

The three-story house at 122 Grant Avenue, just west of
the historic Santa Fe Plaza, was once the epicenter for
some of the most horrific ghostly activity ever reported
in The City Different. The stately colonial style house with a
steeply pitched roof and dormer windows was characteristic

of the homes built by wealthy merchants who moved to New Mexico during the turn of the century. The first accounts I heard about the house — accounts that are repeated by the leaders of various ghost tours — relate that a sickly child lived in the house and cried constantly because he was virtually imprisoned on an upper floor in his wheelchair. One fateful day he rolled his chair too close to a staircase, tumbled down, and died. Other accounts mention a corrupt postal official who did jail time for embezzlement and, after his release, inexplicably was a justice of the peace who married couples at the house. He spent his elder years in a wheelchair.

According to some accounts, the house was vacant for periods of time, yet there were reports of figures standing in the windows. I could find no accounts of horrific murders or other events that would possibly explain what only could be described as a horrific energy contamination of the Grant Avenue House that manifested as a series of terrifying incidents that happened to Artie Garcia over a period of nearly two years.

Garcia, a successful real estate agent, sits down with me in the conference room of the real estate office where he works to tell me about the events that happened to him twenty-seven years previous—events that are still fresh in his mind because of their intense horror. Artie is in his fifties with salt and pepper hair, sparkling eyes, and a playful, smiling almost elfish demeanor. But he becomes very serious when he talks about what happened to him. Even though the event was part of a documentary by the History Channel and has been often repeated, Artie makes it clear that it is not a story he enjoys telling. Indeed, he says he sometimes gets requests to tell the story to schoolchildren particularly around Halloween. "Why?" he wonders. "Why would somebody want me to tell that story to kids? It's difficult enough to tell it to adults and I don't tell it very often." As we settle into chairs, he adds, "It's not like I saw 'Casper the ghost' go through that house. I've always prayed that I would never go through that again."

"I had just moved back to Santa Fe from Seattle," he begins. "My mom knew some people who owned the building," he said, referring to the house at 122 Grant Avenue. "At that point it was an office building. The first floor had a law firm and an insurance company and the second floor belonged to the Chamber Music Festival. The Chamber Music Festival was pretty young at that point and they had the whole second floor. So, the caretakers lived on the third floor. If I moved in I would take care of the building… clean it, take care of it. I would be the janitorial service…and that would pay my rent. I said, 'Well that's a deal, a great deal. Be in downtown Santa Fe. What a deal that was.'"

So, Artie agreed to be the overall caretaker and live-in janitor for the building. He recounts that before moving in, the third floor quarters required a good cleaning. "My mom came with me and we cleaned it all up. The people who had lived there were friends of people my mom knows. And later, down the road—after I moved out—we found out why they moved out so suddenly. For the same reason of what I experienced. But, they never shared that with anybody. One of the things they did tell later was that when they were moving out…. when they packed up their boxes and would go back upstairs to get another load of boxes, the first group of boxes would all be unpacked."

"But the main reason they moved out," Artie pauses and takes a deep breath, "They went in the baby's room and the baby's crib was turned upside down on top of the baby. They moved out overnight, literally."

Not long after Artie moved in, the terrifying events began.

"I used to do some work for the College of Santa Fe with the fraternities. I had gotten back from an event and it was about 11 o'clock at night. I made myself a sandwich and went and sat down to watch this small little TV I had when I heard somebody downstairs."

Artie explains that soon after he moved in, he made an arrangement with the people who worked on the second floor. "There was a door on the second floor. You would open the door and then you went upstairs. The people from Chamber Music worked at night when they were getting the festival ready—they would always knock on the door. They would always knock on the door and tell me that they were there. Or, they would call me. So I called downstairs and I could hear the phone ringing, but no one ever answered. And I could hear footsteps and I could hear doors opening. Because I knew the creaks of the doors already, I knew what door they were opening and where they were. So I could hear the doors opening and closing. I could hear the toilet flush. I got really worried. I thought, somebody's broken in and I don't want to go downstairs."

Quickly, Artie decided that he should turn off the lights in the hallway landing in front of his door because he realized the light might be visible around the closed door on the second floor that opened to the stairs leading up to his room. After he turned off the lights, Artie said, "I heard somebody move the knob. So, at that point, I called my dad." Artie's voice becomes very quiet.

"I got my mom on the phone and I said, let me talk to Dad. She said, 'What's wrong?' and I said, I think somebody's broken in the building. And so she said, 'Do you want him to go over there?' I said, "Yeah, he has to come over here. So I hung up with her."

Artie then begins to explain the terrifying phenomenon that he can describe only as an unnaturally amplified sound. "Maybe two or three minutes later there was this sound. It was so loud. A pounding and like footsteps, slamming of doors... But it was an unnatural sound, unnaturally amplified. Then, it moved up to the roof."

Artie grapples with how to describe the sound, except to repeat that it was "so loud, so amplified" several times. "And it was somehow on both the roof and the second floor at the same time. I called my parents' house again and I said, 'Is Dad there?' and my mom said, 'No, he's on his way and I called your brother. You should be seeing some sort of activity there. And what is that sound?'"

Artie explains that his brother was a Santa Fe City police officer at the time and he was glad his mother had the presence of mind to call him. Artie peeked out the window and could see flashing police lights approaching the house, but the terror was far from over.

"Whatever it was that was on the second floor, went through the door and climbed the steps. I could hear *it* coming up the steps. And at that moment…and this is really hard to believe…and I just hate remembering all this…the temperature of that place dropped. I could see my breath. I had these huge hanging plants in the hallway and all of them froze. They crumpled to the floor. I was watching all this happen while whatever this was was coming up the steps and *it* came around the corner, but I couldn't see *it*. I couldn't see *it*." He swallowing hard before he continues, "The drapes moved. *It* brushed my side. And the stench in there was horrible. And *it* passed me. At that point, I ran down the steps. I don't even remember how I opened the door. I got out of the building."

Artie takes a deep breath and pauses. "And the cops went in there and searched everything and there was nothing wrong. The one thing that they did notice was that my plants were all dead, they were on the floor."

Artie explains that he spent the night at his parent's house, puzzling over what happened and trying to make some sense of it, trying to figure out what *it* was. Still, he decided to go back to the house. "But it happened every night for about a week. It happened between 11 and 1 o'clock. And every night I landed at my parents' house," he says, trying to laugh.

Artie describes how he and his family tried to make sense of the bizarre events. Like many who experience paranormal activities there was confusion, the concerns about what people would think as well as a sense of unreality and disbelief, and of course, speculation about sanity. News spread through the circle of Artie's friends and family. And then, as Arties tells it, "One of the churches got involved. They gave me a call. And, they wanted to talk to me."

Stair landing in Grant Avenue house where plants froze when *it* came up the stairs.

He goes on to explain, "I wasn't really religious. We didn't grow up with religion. My parents always told us that we could choose our own religion. So, I went and met with the priest at one of the parishes and he said, 'Your aunt has indicated to us that you are having some problems at this house that you can't explain.' And I said, I am. Then he asked me odd questions like have I been playing around with organizations that might deal with the occult. I said no. And he asked me my history and I said I did do a paper in college on exorcism." Artie leaned forward and said, "Because I went to a Christian Brother college," as if to explain.

Artie then says that the priest asked if he could come bless the house. "And I said I'm fine with that. I'm fine with that."

Artie confided that the whole idea of a priest coming to his house to bless it or perhaps confront *it* was troubling. "So I asked Jean, my friend from the bank, to come over as a witness because I didn't want to be there by myself." And so began another bizarre chapter in an increasingly bizarre story as Artie explains that even the priest's entry to the house was mysterious. He describes how the house faced a Safeway grocery store parking lot across the street and how the red glow from the sign suffused the house with an eerie glow, making just the setting of the house creepy. Artie and his friend Jean watched as the priest parked across the street in the Safeway lot and got out of his car. To their astonishment, a fog enveloped the priest. And, Artie recalls, "as the priest began to cross the street he actually walked slow motion across that road and came towards the house."

After seeing this strange reality time warp, grossly accentuated by the red glow of the Safeway sign, Artie's friend became worried about what she'd agreed to do. Without reservation, Artie reports, the priest wanted to get started right away...in the basement. The priest began blessing the house. "But," Artie said, "he blessed with a little more terminology than what I was used to hearing in a blessing. And..." There was a long pause while Artie gathered his thoughts. "When he hit the holy water on those walls..." Artie gestures as if shaking a brush, "there were explosions."

"Explosions?" I ask incredulous.

"That's the only way I know to describe it." Artie replies. "Oh my god, it was beyond sound. The sound was so amplified, so loud. Every time the holy water hit the wall there was an explosion." Then he added, "The priest was sweating. I was worried for him."

Artie recalls that the priest finally finished blessing the entire house. "And, for the first time that night I spent the night there. I didn't go to my parents' house. It was peaceful. It was peaceful."

However, Artie's peace was short-lived.

"Other activities started after that," he says, "and I think these were spirits." He speculates, "I think there was something bad there and then there were other spirits that were probably being tormented. That's all I can really think of." Then Artie describes "the talking women" sound phenomenon. He said he could hear two women talking and sometimes laughing and, try as he might, he could never understand what was being said, as if he were listening to a muffled conversation in an adjoining room in which only the cadence of talking came through. "I knew if I was sitting by myself reading, I knew that one or two of them must have been there because I could feel them. And I could hear them. Small talk. But I could never tell what they were saying. Ever! And that used to frustrate me."

And then there were the bed-sitters: "*They* would sit on the corner of the bed. I could feel the corner of the bed go down. And I could see a white shadow moving on the walls. *They* were walking through the room. I was twenty-seven years old, but I was like a kid in my bed…I couldn't get out from under the covers with something sitting on the corner of my bed. I was going, my god, I can't experience this. I've got to keep my eyes open to see if I'm going to touch it. Is it going to touch me? Or, what's going to happen?"

Incredibly, Artie says he lost his fear of the house. "*They* were there with me. They didn't interact. But I knew they were there. I got really comfortable there. I didn't find it threatening anymore." This... despite the fact that *they* apparently didn't like his choice of music sometimes and would scratch the needle across his records. Then there was the time when *they* tried to trap him in a closet.

"It was a closet that connected the kitchen to this one bedroom on the top floor," Artie recalls. "The owners had all their junk in there and some old antiques. I kept those doors closed. And one night I went in there...I just happened to peer in there and there's a light on at the other end. There was no way to get to the closet from the kitchen because there was a sink in front of it. So I crawled through everything to try to turn off that light... and the door slammed shut. I can't even remember how I got out of there, but I did."

Artie was not alone in experiencing strange events. He described how his parents saw strange things at the house when he was gone. "Once I was gone for two weeks out to San Francisco and my parents passed by the house and they would see somebody standing on the right side on that top floor."

I recalled reading accounts of figures seen in the windows when the house was unoccupied.

"In that little dormer thingie?" I ask.

"Yes! Only on that side. My dad would look on the other side. Never saw anything. Only on that one side. But they couldn't tell if it was a man or a woman. It was only a shadow. And, my brother saw it. And my brother said there was a time...a couple nights actually that they would park at the Safeway and they could see the doors opening and closing by themselves because I would leave the lights on in the hallways until I went to bed... but I would be upstairs. And then there were a couple of nights when—literally—all the doors were opening and slamming, the lights were turning off, and the toilets would flush. I could hear people walking up the steps...constantly...and there'd be nobody in the building. I would have to leave the house or go outside and stand on the portal for a while. And then the activity would slow down."

After well over a year of sharing his house with spirits that were at best mischievous and noisy and at worst terrifying in their malevolence, Artie tried having roommates, Ken Smith and Kathy Kline. "Oh, and we got a cat, Missy."

The invisible inhabitants, it seems, did not favor the cat. "Our cat Missy…we found her in the refrigerator. And it looked like maybe it had just happened. She was fine. She was slightly out of it because of the oxygen level. We moved her out of there."

It wasn't long after that Ken and Kathy moved out as well. "They couldn't take it," Artie states, sounding disappointed, adding, "I thought I was nuts. That's what scared me. I was getting kinda pissed at some point. This is not good. I don't want to be here. Friends experienced things when they came over. And it was just weird to see them all go through it too."

It was then that Artie decided it was time to move out.

"And I experienced the box un-packing thing too when I moved out. I would pack my boxes, my books. I'd take a load downstairs and come back and the other boxes would be un-packed. Finally, I had to pack them one-by-one and take them downstairs."

After Artie Garcia moved from the house on 122 Grant Avenue, it was sold to Louise Stewart who turned it into a bed and breakfast she named The Grant Corner Inn. Perhaps the extensive renovation necessary to turn the aging home into a first-rate bed and breakfast swept away or neutralized the negative energies. Unlike reviews of other Santa Fe lodging that tout their ghosts, there is no mention of strange encounters only descriptions of "lush gardens, beautifully appointed guest rooms, fabulous gourmet breakfasts, and the gracious hospitality of Louise and her staff make this an experience not to be missed."

I asked Artie if he ever talked to Louise Stewart, if she ever mentioned strange activity.

"I knew her, but not well. But well enough that we talked. She was a sweet person. They did an article…I want to say six or seven years ago… in *The New Mexican*, before Halloween, and they asked her some questions and she at last said, 'Yes, I hear steps, I hear toilets flush…' and for the first time I felt…" Artie, emotional, gropes for words. "I don't feel like I'm alone. It's a lonely thing when it happens to only you."

The house remained the Grant Corner Inn for twenty plus years. Artie, hyper-knowledgeable about Santa Fe real estate, tells me it was sold to developers who had hoped to "condo-ize" it, but Santa Fe's rigorous zoning laws prohibited that so it was converted to an art gallery.

Even though Artie moved from the house on Grant Avenue, the experience of living there continued to impact his life. And, while he had proclaimed to have finally felt at ease there, his reaction to being asked by a film crew to return to the house seems to indicate otherwise. Artie recounts that in 1996 Warner Brothers came to film a story about the house. "And when we were filming, they could never get the lights bright enough to do anything. We had been experiencing a drought in Santa Fe and it was so hot…and there was a huge clap of lightning as we were walking into the house. Just bizarre. And the guys…you've never seen these guys jump so high in your life. I'll never forget that. It was hilarious. Then three years ago they came back and did a new interview. But I didn't enter the house. I haven't entered the house since…" his voice trails off and then he continues. "I stayed on the main floor, I didn't go up stairs…I didn't want to go upstairs."

And then there were the dreams—the dreams that haunted him for many years. Dreams, he says, that only recently stopped. "I had dreams for about sixteen years about a specific house and the things that were going on in it. And it was not good."

"Were the dreams about the house?" I ask. "Was it like a post-traumatic stress nightmare where you continued to relive the event?"

"Oh, it was a horrible nightmare. It was about…I was protecting all these people and I could not see whatever *it* was, but *it* was horrible."

There was that reference again. That *it*.

"*It* was in the back part of the house."

"So, the house in your dream wasn't the same house?" I persist.

"Not the same house, but the rooms are similar. Same kind of Victorian. And I can walk through that house and tell you those rooms and there's similar rooms in the Grant Street house, but it's not the same house as in the dream," Artie says.

"Could it have been the house as it was?" I wondered.

"It could have been. But I never did see the outside. It's always inside."

"If I could describe the dream to you…" Artie pauses, groping for words. "It's horrific. I'm literally yelling in this dream. For the goodness of saving something… And there are times when I'm yelling with hands straight up. And I scream, 'God commands you!'" Artie raises his hands over his head to demonstrate. "And I'll wake up with my arms over my head."

"Sometimes I'm protecting my mom and my dad and my brother and sometimes I'm protecting our pets. It's like I'm constantly having to fight and protect from something bad or evil or whatever. And then I wondered if I should go get the dream analyzed, but I never did, and I don't know what they would think." Artie laughs, trying to lighten the mood and refers to the house aspect of the dream. "Other than I thought that maybe because I'm a realtor, maybe I'm having some anxiety. But I don't know. I love my job."

Artie says he eventually decided to confront the terror in his dreams. "I worked on it because I tired of being in that same situation, in that same predicament. So, I opened that door and *it* comes towards me. And I think I've won because I wake up not tired…I wake up thinking I've satisfied something."

Since some people are more receptive, more able to perceive the supernatural I ask Artie about his upbringing—if he had any other paranormal experiences.

"My upbringing? I used to spend my summers and my holidays with my grandmother in Alcalde [a tiny village in Northern New Mexico]. And there's a lot of witchcraft in those towns. We never experienced the witchcraft." Artie pauses and then adds, "But we did see some weird balls of fire along the ditch. That could have been electrical for all we know," he adds, laughing.

I ask what he means about 'not experiencing the witchcraft.'

"My grandmother told us stories when we were children of a witch…a witch that died in Alcalde. And we were always told to be careful with specific people in the village and never take food from them and to never let them touch our hair. And certain things like that and we would obey that. And so we learned all about that as children."

I wonder if it was perhaps his grandmother's influence that made him more receptive to paranormal events and ask him to tell me if there were any other strange experiences he can remember from childhood.

He recalls that, "Once when my brother was really small, we were in the kitchen and right outside the door we could hear some galoshes walking in the mud because it was raining outside. My grandmother went to the door to look outside." Artie gestures with his hands, drawing an imaginary diagram on the table. "All of the house was connected. There was an *estensa*… which is like a storeroom… and there were rubber boots in there facing the corner. And the next day we learned one of her cousins that lived in one of the houses had passed away. And that's the connection because those were his rubber boots. So that's the only other experience I can tell you I had as a kid."

Artie reflects on life with his grandmother. "My grandmother was a curandera [healer]. I sliced my arm up once and she went for this specific mud. She got the mud from the ditch. It had like grass in it and all that and she put it on, caked it on. It worked! The next day it was scabbed over and healing. She was great. She knew what she was doing. We learned everything from her. We learned how to cook. She baked out in the *horno* [outdoor adobe oven]."

I remark that it sounds like his grandmother was very influential in his life and that childhood in a small northern New Mexico village, so steeped in history and folklore, must have been fascinating.

Artie replies, "We were so lucky! That was last of that generation of old ways." Then, he launches into another story about his grandmother confronting penitentes, a very secretive Catholic brotherhood found only in northern New Mexico with roots in the thousand-year-old secret societies that practiced self-flagellation.

He recalls how he and his brother "were sitting with my uncles in the *morada* [windowless, secret meeting house]. The men were whipping themselves and praying and chanting and smoking." For emphasis he exclaims, "Smoking!" and shakes his head. He continues, "Suddenly, the two doors opened... just whapped right open and hit the sides of the wall. And we're just sitting there on the bench looking...and it's my grandmother who is 4'9."

"Aren't women strictly forbidden from ever setting foot in a morada?" I ask.

"Yes, she's not allowed in there. She yells at my uncles, 'Where are the boys?' So we're sitting there... She goes in there, grabs us, and gets us out and slams those doors shut."

Artie and I laugh together at the thought of this tiny woman bursting into a morada and challenging the most sacrosanct and secret fraternity in New Mexico by plucking out her grandsons.

"She was a powerful lady," Artie says, adding that wasn't the only time she challenged long-held traditions. "The women are supposed to carry the big statue of Jesus on Good Friday. And she said, 'We're not doing it. The women are not doing it. You guys do it.' She said, 'The women are not your slaves. You do it.' She was changing the mentality of the ritual. And we got to experience that."

When I remark that it seems like his grandmother might have influenced his perceptions of the supernatural, he continues to insist that she hasn't.

"Did that influence it? I don't think so."

I ask him what the lasting impact has been: does he feel like it made him a more spiritual or less skeptical person.

"I think so, very much so, and those dreams have made me even more. It altered my life and I think it was meant to be. I think it was meant to be."

I am so captivated and stunned by Artie's story that I want to learn everything I can about the house at 122 Grant Avenue. It had gone through several owners and was once, as Artie mentioned, a bed and breakfast. Today it houses the Andrew Smith Gallery that specializes in high-end photographic art. Or, as the sign outside proclaims: "Masterpieces of Photography."

The Andrew Smith Gallery employees graciously allow me to wander around the old house—even the top floor that is closed off to gallery patrons. The house has been beautifully refurbished and renovated with a careful eye to preserving its charm. The windows on the upper floors still have the wavy old glass with ripples and imperfections; the oak banisters are polished to a high shine. I look at the landing that Artie Garcia described as the place where he hung plants—the plants that were inexplicably frozen by *it.* There is a window at the end of the landing that illuminates the area and it's easy to imagine that it would be great place for hanging plants.

In its current life as an art gallery, all the walls of the Grant Avenue House are painted in soft neutral tones. The wall colors and the precisely placed lighting show off the stunning photography for which the gallery is renown.

As I stand in the charming dormer nook, I try to feel if anything evil or sinister is there. It feels relaxing, even peaceful. The remodeling and refurbishing must have changed the energy. I ask people working there if they have heard the stories…if anything strange has happened. They were familiar with the stories of "some kind of haunting." A young woman tells me that early one morning the intercom lines suddenly started ringing on all the phones. When she picked up one phone, there was only a hissing or whooshing sound. She said that she and the other people working laughed and said, "Maybe it's the ghosts." Then she added, "It *was* kind of weird."

A manager, sitting at a desk, shakes his head in disbelief and remarks that, as a Santa Fe native, he's not sure when the haunting could have happened. He takes a newspaper clipping out of a drawer and, pointing to an article, says, "Here's some real history." I note several of the names in the article and decide to dig a little further. I want to know the history of the house. Who was the crippled child? Was there a crippled child? Who might have had a profound attachment to the house, so profound as to manifest such havoc? What was the real story of the house?

The relatives of the original owner of the home would provide fascinating information that did not include stories of a crippled child tumbling down the stairs and demonstrate once again how the original seed of a story can become completely distorted into a strange tale completely unrelated, and actually in some ways, less fascinating than the real story.

Raymond and Betty Kirsting have a keen interest in the Grant Avenue house and the telling of the "true story" of the house's history. That's because Raymond Kirsting's mother, Mary, grew up in the house and Raymond grew up in a house next door to it, which would later be razed to make room for the Georgia O'Keefe Museum. The Kirstings compiled a detailed history of what happened in the house from the time the house was built by Mr. Kirsting's grandmother, Ada Peacock Moore, until it was sold at auction in 1950.

J. G. Trimble sold the lot on which the house would be built to Alois Renehan for the astonishing price of $10 in 1902. Renehan resold it in 1906 — to Ada Moore — for $100. Contrary to all the stories that state the house was built in 1905, the Kirstings have a 1910 census report that shows no house at the corner of Grant Avenue and Johnson Street. The 1910 and 1911 tax assessment valued the "lot" at $150. However, the 1912 tax assessment valued the "lot and house" at $1,060.

Ada Peacock Moore was the wife of Reverend William Hayes Moore, a prominent pastor, who moved his wife and young daughter, Etta, from Doylestown, Pennsylvania in 1897 to lead the First Presbyterian Church in Santa Fe. Reverend Moore was one of the many thousands of "tuberculosis immigrants," people who came to New Mexico from the turn of the century until the

The Grant House sometime in the 1920s. *Courtesy of Raymond and Betty Kirsting.*

1940s hoping the dry climate and clear air would cure them of "the consumption." Prior to their move to New Mexico, the Moores lost two children in infancy. Three more daughters were born to the Moores after they moved to New Mexico: Ruth, Jessie, who died in infancy, and Mr. Kirsting's mother, Mary.

Reverend Moore died in 1904, leaving his widow with three small girls to raise. The Kirstings believe that Reverend Moore's family were "people of means" and that the three young Moore girls received an inheritance that Ada Peacock Moore used to build the house on Grant Avenue. Ada married Arthur E. P. Robinson in 1909, a man twenty years her junior, and the Kirstings speculate that he had been a construction worker on the house although Robinson was listed in the 1910 census as working for the railroad.

Robinson also worked as a clerk at the post office and it was in this job that he ran afoul of the law. According to the Kirstings, it was Robinson's job to send the reel of movie film from the Santa Fe movie house to Denver each week. He used previously cancelled stamps to do this and was convicted of postal fraud, but never, contrary to some reports, served any jail time. He later

Ada Peacock Moore in 1897.
Courtesy of Raymond and Betty Kirsting.

delivered the *Denver Post* and became a justice of the peace.

Ada, an 1884 graduate of the Philadelphia Conservatory of Music, taught piano lessons and held piano recitals in the living room. Betty Kirsting points to a lovely basket on a shelf and said, "An Indian family paid Ada with that basket for teaching their child [to play the] piano." Ever the entrepreneur, Ada also operated the home as a rooming house and Mr. Kirsting remembers a sort of bed and breakfast for tourists with a sign on the front porch welcoming travelers. Betty Kirsting speculates that women from rural areas might have come to the home to have their babies delivered by a local doctor because they have met several people over the years who claim they were born in the house.

According to Raymond Kirsting, the three Moore girls had the third floor of the house all to themselves and his mother's room was on the west side of the house. It had a tiny balcony that was later converted to a fire escape.

Mr. Kirsting describes how his older cousins "had no use for" Robinson, calling him Uncle Booby. However, Mr. Kirsting found no reason to dislike Robinson, whom he called Uncle Bobby. He recalled that when Ada suffered a stroke in 1937, Robinson cared for her tenderly and had a small addition put on the house on the first floor since the stroke so incapacitated her she needed to use a wheelchair. Mr. Kirsting recalled that a bell call system

Arthur E. P. Robinson dressed up for Santa Fe Fiesta.
Courtesy of Raymond and Betty Kirsting.

was set up between the two houses so that Mr. Kirsting's mother, Mary, could be summoned to help Ada.

Mr. Kirsting described Robinson as "a character." According to local lore he was a beloved justice of the peace because he never sent anyone to jail and married couples in the parlor of the Grant Avenue house. Every Christmas he would erect a huge, elaborately decorated tree that would span the front two rooms of the house. Oddly, he would always lop the top off the tree and erect it as sort of a miniature Christmas tree on the upstairs sleeping porch on the west side of the house. He would leave the tree up until his birthday at the end of January and this eccentricity was the subject of teasing in the local paper. Mr. Kirsting also marveled over another of Robinson's quirks. After Ada's stroke, Robinson slept on the second floor porch even in the dead of winter. Santa Fe winters can be brutally cold with temperatures dipping to zero or below at night. Mr. Kirsting also marveled over Robinson's gardening skills, recalling that he had a huge stand of dahlias and a lovely grape arbor in the back yard of the Grant Avenue house. Growing dahlias in New Mexico requires an extraordinary amount of effort and dedication.

Ada Peacock Moore in the 1930s with one of her dogs. According to Raymond Kirsting, she "always" had a dog. *Courtesy of Raymond and Betty Kirsting.*

Robinson dug up the tubers every fall and carefully stored them in the basement, replanting them again each spring.

When Ada died in 1944, Robinson and each of Ada's daughters received one-quarter ownership of the house. Interestingly, while Robinson's name appeared on the tax rolls for the Grant Avenue house, Ada never granted him ownership. The house was always her sole property. The daughters sold their claim to the house to Robinson. He later remarried—a much younger woman—and the house passed to his widow in 1952. After Ada's death, claims against the property mounted and, to settle them, Robinson's widow auctioned it in 1953.

I relate several incidents from Artie Garcia's story to the Kirstings, specifically the part where Artie said he could hear two women talking and laughing but he could never hear what they were saying. Mr. Kirsting looks thoughtful and then recalls that his mother and her sister Ruth were "best friends, very, very close" and that they did spend a lot of time talking and laughing in their rooms on the third floor. Tragically, Mr. Kirsting's mother was killed in an automobile accident in 1971. And, he adds wistfully, "I wish I'd asked her more about all the things that happened at the house when she was young."

Grant Avenue House showing the second floor sleeping porch (left side of photo), where Robinson slept even in the winter. *Courtesy Raymond and Betty Kirsting.*

The Grant Avenue House from the same angle as it is today.

Obviously all the legends of the early days of the Grant Avenue house are greatly distorted. The Kirstings' accounts of what actually happened during the first fifty years of the Grant Avenue home are a sharp contrast to the most often told version of the story:

"Unfortunately for the young couple, shortly after they built their new home, a sickly son was born who required constant attention. To make matters worse, the woman's husband died shortly thereafter. The young mother soon remarried a man who was said to have not been a very nice person. Over the years, the child continued to get worse and the mother threw herself into caring for the young boy. During this time, visitors to the home would often report hearing the young boy crying and banging on the walls of his upstairs room while his mother was downstairs visiting. Confined to a wheelchair, the boy was said to have continually rolled too close to the stairway, tumbling down, wheelchair and all, to the landing below. The child finally died of his ailments and the woman and her husband moved away."

So, the seeds of truth of this story are that Ada Peacock Moore did have an ill child, a girl, who died. However, the child never lived in the Grant Avenue house. And, while some of Mr. Kirsting's cousins may not have fond memories of Ada Moore's second husband, he could hardly be described as "not a very nice person," considering he attentively cared for his bedridden wife for many years.

Betty Kirsting believes the Grant Avenue house should be known as the Ada Peacock Moore house and indeed that seems very appropriate. The real story of the resilient, resourceful widow who taught piano lessons and ran a rooming house and her eccentric, much younger second husband is actually more fascinating than the sensationalized and very negative legends.

As for the horrifying and strange things that happened to Artie, those stories are real too. Lingering energies manifesting in territorial and terrifying ways and then eventually transforming? It's all part of the mystery.

THE PLAYFUL
CHILD GHOST

In one of my earliest ghost story hunts it seemed that sometimes the ghosts had their own agendas. It was as if simply by seeking to tell their stories I was influenced by them and led in different places than I had originally intended, like some quirky version of quantum mechanics where the very act of observing changes what is observed. For instance, I had prepared very carefully for one ghost story hunting trip to Santa Fe. I went over my notes and the places I planned to visit from my research about ghostly sightings. I printed maps of the locations and stuck them in the three-ring binder with my research notes.

I decided my first destination would be "The Oldest House," an ancient adobe structure that is documented as the oldest house in the United States in terms of European settlement.

I packed up my shoulder bag with notebook, pens, and tape recorder and grabbed my camera. I loaded my golden retriever Jupiter into the truck and plugged in my iPod for proper road music.

As I neared Santa Fe, I reached into my bag on the seat next to me for the binder with the maps. I groped with my hand, but couldn't find it. I was incredulous, certain that I could not have forgotten it. I pulled into a shopping center parking lot and grabbed my bag into my lap and stared dumbfounded into its depths. Ah, it must have slipped down between the seat and the door because of course I couldn't possibly have forgotten it…again nothing. I couldn't believe it. I had driven forty miles to Santa Fe before I realized I didn't have the essential information I needed—especially the maps. As a Spanish colonial settlement turned city, Santa Fe has labyrinthine roads that curve and twist around, streets that inexplicably change names from one block to the next, as well as from two-way to one-way. Even as a native New Mexican who has been to Santa Fe hundreds of times, I always managed to get lost or turned around. Maps are essential.

I pulled back onto St. Francis Drive, one of Santa Fe's main drags, and just began driving around aimlessly trying to make sense of how I could possibly have forgotten the binder. For no particular reason, I turned onto Paseo de Peralta. I spotted the tiny religious articles shop down Old Santa Fe Trail, where, eight years before, I had purchased a window sticker of Our Lady of Guadalupe for my then-new truck. While traveling in Mexico, I developed a great fondness for Our Lady of Guadalupe after seeing the many colorful shrines devoted to her tucked into all manner of places from alleyways to a rock in the middle of the desert.

I turned around and headed back to Old Santa Fe Trail. Maybe I was supposed to just wing it and figure things out as I went along. Maybe, when pursuing ghost stories, it might be better to let the stories find me.

The Old Santa Fe Trail Gift Shop and Religious Articles is a tiny shop packed with racks of prayer cards, crosses, tiny bejeweled shrines, and all manner of Catholic religious items. Presiding over the colorful clutter is Connie Hernandez, a tiny woman with a warm smile and a demeanor that radiates kindness, wisdom, and welcome to all. Her shop is so packed with unique merchandise it is nearly impossible to find anything, and that of course gives Connie the opportunity to provide personal attention. I inquire about a specific Our Lady of Guadalupe window sticker that I had bought many years before. I describe what the sticker looked like and, using my hands as a template, I show her the size. "It was oval-shaped," I say. From some reason, perhaps because of her friendliness and motherly concern, I feel compelled to tell her that it had adorned the windshield of my truck, and that after a wreck, the windshield had to be replaced. She nods sympathetically and asks me how many I want. "Four," I reply. She disappears in the back and returns with four stickers. However, they are not the ones I was looking for. While they are oval shaped, they're larger and much more showy and festooned with glitter. I shake my head and tell her that the one I had was transparent and rather simple. She points to a totally bleached out version of my sticker in her shop window. "Like that?" she asks. "Yes, that's it." She frowns, "Hmmm, I haven't sold those in a very, very long time. Perhaps I should order more." She turns to a small plastic box with drawers and withdraws the stickers. "I'm almost out," she announces.

As I complete my purchase, I ask her, "Where exactly is the Oldest House from here?" She takes me out to the street and points out its location several blocks north. I explain that I'm writing a book about Santa Fe ghosts and that the Oldest House has a history of interesting stories. She nods, yes, so she's heard. "And do you have any interesting ghost stories?" I ask.

"No, not me personally, but I can tell you something very strange that happened just up the street." She turns and points to the south. "Just a few houses up. It's State offices now, but it used to be a restaurant." We go inside and I get out my notebook and begin scribbling.

"It was a long time ago," she begins. "Gosh, more than thirty years probably. It was Ernie's Restaurant, but before that it was a private home. There was an old man who lived there, Mr. Umberhine. He wandered around the neighborhood with an old camera without film in it saying he was taking pictures. People said he used to be a photographer. He was a little crazy. Anyway, people say his little sister died in that house. After he passed away, it became Ernie's Restaurant. The waitresses there said that sometimes they'd see a little girl. You know, kind of a fleeting glimpse. But the strangest part was that they couldn't keep their aprons on. Even if they tied them in front with a double square knot...all of a sudden the apron would just come untied."

Connie smiled and said, "So that's the only real story I know. I think the little girl was maybe trapped in Purgatory, was a restless soul."

I decide to research the Umberhine family, but about all I could find is references to several graves at Santa Fe's old Fairview Cemetery for an I. M. Umberhine, Emil Dexter Umberhine, and Lloyd Umberhine. Cemetery records for the National Cemetery have listed an Army veteran, Rush D. Umberhine, who was born October 31, 1895 and died April 30, 1979. Maybe I. M. Umberhine was the little girl.

I wanted to find out.

Fairview Cemetery is on busy Cerrillos Road in the center of Santa Fe. It is a very old cemetery with a few scraggly drought-tolerant trees. There are no manicured lawns, no sprinklers, just dirt and dust. By New Mexico old dirt cemetery standards, Fairview is quite austere. Many old dirt cemeteries in New Mexico have colorfully decorated graves that look like scale model replicas of Pasadena Rose Parade floats perched in the dirt. Festooned with rafts of neon-bright polyester and plastic flowers, shiny mylar balloons, pinwheels, and, sadly in the case of small children, teddy bears or other toys, the graves—even old graves—are often tended regularly. Some graves in the dirt old cemeteries also have small wire fences around them as if to keep the more rowdy dead penned in for eternity.

There are few bright flowers at Fairview and many very solemn granite headstones poking up through the weeds and dirt along with the odd tree-shaped marker for a "Woodman of the World" and a giant granite boulder with "Here Lies Eliza" and some sort of cryptic carving...and nothing else.

Finding the Umberhine graves proved to be no easy task. First, the grave map at the front of Fairview designates different sections, alphabetically labeled like stadium seating. Numbers marks the individual graves on the map. A huge book lists the residents in alphabetical order with their section and grave number. The trouble is that there are no obvious alphabetical letters on the various sections of the cemetery making it necessary to plot a course through the cemetery by finding a particularly large or gaudy marker to use as a landmark, noting the name on the grave, and going to the grave book to look up the name to determine the resident's location. As I search through the cemetery, plotting my course by the larger grave markers, I find myself obsessed with finding I. M. Umberhine, expecting to find one of the small, poignant marble lambs that mark so many of the children's graves.

When I finally find the Umberhine family plot, I discover something interesting. I. M. is Ina May Umberhine...except she hardly died as a child: she was born August 14, 1862 and died July 18, 1943 at age 81. Next to her lie Lloyd, born February 24, 1893 and died December 24, 1928 at age 31, and Emil Dexter, born November 17, 1902, died December 15, 1981 at age 79. From the dates it looks like Lloyd and Emil are her sons (as was, likely, Rush who was buried at the veteran's cemetery). So, I've gotten no answers—only more questions. Like, where was *Mr.* Umberhine? If he wasn't buried with them, or from what I could determine, anywhere in Santa Fe, maybe a daughter could be buried elsewhere as well?

Now that the little girl is even more of a mystery, I decide to visit the scene of the haunting—the old Umberhine house. Currently, 613 Old Santa Fe Trail is the home of the New Mexico Association of Counties. From the street the historical looking one-story—what I would call, Victorian adobe—looks like a carefully restored old house with an inviting white front door with a large oval window. However, there is an extensive addition in the back—nearly invisible from the street—that makes it an office building.

I venture in, introduce myself to the receptionist, and tell her the story of the playful little girl said to haunt the premises

The former Umberhine house is now offices for the New Mexico Association of Counties.

and ask her if there have been any strange occurrences in the building.

She tells me to call next week and talk to her boss because she's not sure if anybody can talk to me. When I contact her boss by phone, I tell him that strange things have been reported to have happened in that building. "Yes," he says laughing, "but fortunately not to me." He says he'll send out an email to all his staff because "I know some of them have experienced some strange things, and we'll see if anybody wants to be interviewed."

Unfortunately, nobody does. However, the vague references make me think that the little girl may still be playing tricks and maybe the encounters have been more personal than some people would feel discussing with a stranger.

SAN MIGUEL MISSION

S an Miguel is regarded as the oldest church in the United States. The Holy Trinity (Old Swedes) Church in Wilmington, Delaware, built in 1699 (a full hundred years after the construction of San Miguel), takes exception to the oldest church designation, smugly appending the description, "the nation's oldest church building still standing as originally built" to its title.

Still, there is no doubt that San Miguel has a much longer history in terms of a location of power and worship. That's because there are two intertwining stories of San Miguel Mission: its long, colorful, and sometimes violent history as the oldest church in the United States; and its mystical history as an ancient Native American power spot, a center of concentrated paranormal activity, and, perhaps, one point on a triangular vortex of earth energy that encompasses several ancient structures in close proximity to each other.

Of course the concept of an energy vortex is as controversial and un-provable by existing technology as ghosts are and most people scoff at the idea as New Age nonsense. Energy vortex or not, San Miguel has remained at the center of centuries of conflict, controversy, and devotion. And, as its fascinating history demonstrates, San Miguel seems to be a magnet for the devoted, the powerful, and the bizarre. Its construction,

San Miguel Mission, the oldest church in the United States.

subsequent partial destructions and resurrections, and controversies are like a microcosm of New Mexico's long and colorful history.

If one thing is certain about the history of New Mexico's earliest colonization, in which San Miguel figures so prominently, it is disagreement among historians. Some say that the first colonization expedition led by Don Juan de Oñate into the geographic region that would become New Mexico numbered two hundred; others say as many as six hundred. Likely the number was somewhere around four hundred, consisting of about three hundred soldiers and their wives and children. Some accounts say eight Franciscan friars and priests accompanied the expedition; others say ten. Oddly, all accounts are consistent about the massive number of animals the expedition brought: 7,000 head of livestock that included oxen, sheep, swine, cows, goats, horses, donkeys, and mules.

While the majority of Oñate's entourage had sold everything they owned in order to participate in the expedition, one of Oñate's captains must have been – to use the quaint old expression – something of a dandy. This particular captain had twenty-two wagons to carry a wardrobe rivaling that of a modern day rock star: imported satin and velvet clothes, plumed and tasseled hats, leather boots, and gloves. Then there was the captain's hand-carved bed, mattresses, and linens plus fine equestrian bling for his horses. All this bumping over rutted wagon paths, through blistering deserts, engulfed in clouds of dust kicked up by the hoofed glacier of plodding livestock.

Some accounts say the expedition of eighty-three ox-carts, twenty-four wagons, Oñate's two personal carriages, assorted military and mining equipment, and of course the livestock, stretched for two miles (others say four) when it set off from Santa Barbara in southern Chihuahua, Mexico on January 26, 1598.

After a harrowing trip through the Chihuahuan desert, Oñate stopped at the Rio Grande near present day El Paso. Spaniards, being quite the legal aficionados, followed precise procedures laid out by royal lawyers for claiming land that involved formal declarations, complete with signatory witnesses. Oñate read *La Toma* (the taking), a declaration that all land drained by the Great River – from the leaves of the trees in the forest to the stones and sands of the river – to be the possession of King Philip II of Spain. With a fanfare of trumpets and volleys of musket shots, Oñate affixed the Royal Standard and a cross to a living tree, completing the legal requirements of *La Toma* that would warm the hearts of the royal lawyers. Regarding *La Toma*, Oñate wrote, "Another reason (for the conquest of New Mexico) is the need for correcting and punishing the sins against nature and against humanity which exist among these bestial nations and which it behooves my King and Prince as a most powerful lord to correct and repress...Another reason is the great number of children born among these infidel people who neither recognize nor obey their true God and Father."

One curious omission in the various accounts of the Oñate expedition is the population of Indian "servants." Sometimes they were referred to as servants and sometimes "Indian allies." But the odd twist is that they weren't indigenous to the Southwest, but rather to Mexico. They were Tlaxcalan Indians and the official historical information for San Miguel Mission puts their number at around seven hundred. If that seems a bizarre disproportion of servants to masters, that's because of the unlikely alliance the Tlaxcalans had formed with the Spanish decades earlier, an alliance in which they traded freedom for protection when a Tlaxcalan leader recognized that aligning his forces with the Spanish would be of great benefit to his people in their on-going struggles with their bitter enemy, the Aztec, who periodically raided the Tlaxcalans for human sacrifice victims. So, formed a classic *the enemy of my enemy is my friend* allegiance that many historians believe it to be one of the defining events in Mexican history. And, in terms of a disproportionate number of servants to masters, seven hundred servants is still only one servant to manage one hundred head of livestock.

When Oñate's expedition finally reached northern New Mexico, they settled in the Tewa pueblo Ohkay Owingeh (place of the strong people) and changed its name to "San Juan." Initially, the Ohkay Owningeh people welcomed Oñate and his expedition, generously sharing their limited provisions and space. Meanwhile, the Tlaxcalans were relegated to the area that would become Santa Fe in a place called the Barrio de Analco (neighborhood beyond the river).

The Christianized Tlaxcalans immediately began construction on a *hermita* (primitive shrine) in 1598. They built it on top of an ancient subterranean Indian ceremonial structure called a kiva. Archeological evidence dates the last use of the kiva at around 1300 A.D. More than a decade after their first building efforts, the Tlaxcalans, under the directions of what one account describes as "zealous" Franciscan Friars, expanded the original building in 1610, completing it over the next several decades as a massive-walled church. Both the Tlaxcalans and Spanish soldiers worshiped at the mission. Later, a military infirmary staffed by the Friars was constructed next to the mission on the south side.

Not long after its completion, the first of several bizarre incidents took place related to power struggles between the military and the Franciscan Friars. Spanish governor Felipe Sotelo Ossario was brought before the Inquisition for interrupting a church service when he berated his officers for not standing at attention when he arrived late for Sunday Mass. Another Governor, Luis de Rosas, feuded with the Franciscans and, when two Friars arrived unannounced to meet with him in an attempt to resolve the dispute, he had them beaten. Governor Rosas was in turn excommunicated. He retaliated by stealing the mission bells, burning down the infirmary, and threatening to burn down the entire church. Rosas was then arrested by his own troops and jailed. Before he could be sent to Mexico City for trial, an angry mob stormed the jail and killed him.

However, the most harrowing event in the mission's long history, and certainly one likely to result in restless spirits, occurred during the Pueblo Revolt of 1680 when between eighty to one hundred Tlaxcalans perished and the mission was nearly destroyed.

The Pueblo Revolt, a universal uprising of all indigenous people against Spanish rule in New Mexico, was a major event in Southwest, and U.S., history and its historical interpretation is contentious even today in New Mexico. Descendants of Spanish settlers consider it a massacre; the Native people, a revolt against religious oppression. Historically, it was the most successful Native uprising in all of North America—ever. It was instigated by an Ohkay Owingeh shaman Po'pay (sometimes written Popé). After accusations that he was a sorcerer and practiced idolatry, Po'pay was imprisoned, suffered a public beating, and, according to some accounts, even survived a hanging in 1675 for violating the Spanish ban on Native religious practices. Po'pay fled his Ohkay Owingeh home to Taos Pueblo, where he spent five years plotting an uprising against the Spanish.

Despite sometimes vast distances between pueblos, as well as differences in language, Po'pay united indigenous people, including some Apaches—bitter enemies of the pueblo people—to revolt against the Spanish on August 11, 1680. The countdown "clock" consisted of knotted yucca fiber ropes carried by runners to all pueblos up and down the Rio Grande corridor and as far away as Zuni—some two hundred miles to the south. Pueblo leaders were informed by the runners to untie one knot a day until all knots were untied. On that day they were to overthrow the Spaniards in their respective communities knowing that the same thing was occurring simultaneously in all other Native communities. If they did not overthrow the Spaniards, other Pueblo people would invade their village and destroy it.

As the revolt unfolded, the Tlaxcalans—men, women, and children—barricaded themselves behind the seemingly impenetrable earthen walls of San Miguel. But the pueblo warriors climbed to the roof of the nearby two-story "Oldest House," north of San Miguel, and shot flaming arrows through the tiny upper windows of the church into the dry roof timbers. According to accounts, the screams of those trapped inside could be heard as far away as the Palace of the Governors as the roof collapsed in flames on them. The Pueblo Revolt lasted eight days and all Spanish citizens and the surviving Tlaxcalans fled the city of Santa Fe for Cuidad Juarez, three hundred miles to the south.

The Spanish returned to Santa Fe some twelve years later (two years after Po'pay died) and recaptured the city. Governor General Don Diego de Vargas ordered the immediate repair and restoration of San Miguel Mission. However the work was not completed for another seventeen years. After its rededication in 1710, San Miguel served as military chapel and then fell into disrepair in a complicated history of ownership. There were subsequent attempts to revive the structure, including the addition of a triple-tiered bell tower and alter screen in the late 1700s. In 1859 Bishop Jean Baptiste Lamy—a cleric who figures prominently in several of the stories in this book—purchased the Chapel and its land for the De La Salle Christian Brothers, a religious community of lay brothers, founded by French Priest Saint Jean-Baptiste de la Salle, who devote their lives to the Christian education of the poor. To make San Miguel a more comfortable place to worship and to prepare it for use as a boy's school, the De La Salle Christian Brothers covered the bull's blood-hardened mud floors with wood and added an altar rail and new doors.

Then, in a most bizarre twist of fate, San Miguel was seriously damaged again in 1872. Some accounts cite an earthquake, others a terrible storm that toppled the bell towers. With no funds to undertake the serious repairs necessary to keep the structure safe and functional, the Brothers made the difficult decision in 1887 to tear down the venerable old mission. But Santa Fe rallied around its beloved landmark. Volunteers began the exhausting work of restoring San Miguel and people even came from surrounding areas to help with the project. Two giant stone buttresses were constructed to stabilize the massive walls. The interior and exterior were re-plastered and a tar and gravel roof replaced the leaky mud roof. A more modest bell tower was added and, later, additional buttresses to insure stability. The small windows on the north side, perhaps in memory of flaming arrows, were sealed off and plastered over.

So, with that long, colorful, sometimes violent history, it's no surprise that strange sightings and ghostly activities are reported at and around San Miguel and the "Oldest House." Employees at the State of New Mexico offices – a building only several feet to the east of the church – report a man dressed all in black and presumed to be a priest roaming the halls. A small gift shop adjoins the church on the site of the burned infirmary. It was once a private residence and there are stories of appearances of a small child, presumably a youngster who died there in the 1940s.

Today, San Miguel is accessed not through the front doors, but through the gift shop attached to the south side of the mission. Before I go in, I stand outside and try to get a sense of anything unusual. Nothing. I step inside. Next to the doorway that leads from the gift shop into the church, a man with a large cross around his neck sits reading a prayer book. He greets me warmly when I come in the door, recites a brief history of the church, and invites me to go into inside for the modest admission charge of one dollar. I tell him that I do want to look in the church because I've heard that strange things have happened in there. I tell him about my quest for Santa Fe ghosts, hand him my card as a matter of introduction, and ask him if he's had any experiences.

Richard Lindsley carefully puts a marker in his book and places it on a shelf under the cash register. "Yes, yes I have had some experiences." He explained he's been the gift shop curator and church caretaker for a little over a year. After only about a month on the job, when walking back into the gift shop after tending the candles in the church, he suddenly felt chilled to the bone. "I knew," he said solemnly, "that this is *their* place and I must let it be as that and accept *them*. It is *their* place."

Richard then recalled that about six months prior a youth about sixteen years old came into the shop from the church.

Giant stone buttresses were installed by volunteers to prevent the collapse of San Miguel.

"He had a hard time talking to me, much the way young people do when talking to—(air quotes)—old people." We laugh. "The young man seemed rather agitated," he went on. "He asked me how to get up to the choir loft. I explained that there is really no way to get up there now, that it's filled with heating equipment and ductwork, but that in old days, the Indians used a ladder to get to the choir loft. 'But how do you get up there?' he asked again. And again I explained that it was inaccessible now. But he kept persisting in asking me how to get up there and I got rather exasperated because he asked me over and over. Finally he said, 'There's a man up there, dressed in black' and he wanted to go up and see him."

"That's really all that's happened to me here," Richard concluded, but added, "If you're interested and have some time, I can tell you something really amazing that happened to me when I worked as the curator of The Loretto Chapel." *[Described in The Loretto Chapel chapter.]*

Richard attends to several visitors who have entered the gift shop while I review my notes. While almost reluctant to comment at first, Mr. Lindsley now seems eager to share more insights regarding the mysteries of ghosts, spirits, or unseen entities. He tells me that most of the paranormal activity around San Miguel seemed to take place at 10 a.m. and that the boy who had seen the mysterious man in black had seen the apparition around 10 a.m.

"You know the priest who says mass here, Father Ricardo Russo, is really a man's man. He is not one to take to flights of fancy. He's the chaplain for the National Guard and the Brothers hired him to say mass. I met him a few times when I had my dog at the dog park. Once when I mentioned paranormal events [at San Miguel], he said very matter-of-factly, 'That place has many strange things going on…many.'" Mr. Lindsley looked very thoughtful and then continued, "You don't pump a man like that with questions. Those few words spoke volumes."

Richard goes on to tell me that Brother Lester Lewis, San Miguel Mission Curator, was contacted by, "A New Age," he grapples with the description, "Spiritualist? Psychic? Well, whatever she was… For what it's worth, she told Brother Lester that there is a triangular vortex between San Miguel, the Oldest House, and a gift shop [now an art gallery] across the street. All these places are owned by the Christian Brothers. Brother Lester said she told him she saw a very dark and angry soul in one of the rooms of the gift shop across the street, a spirit that gives you a chill. Anyway, the spiritualist, or whatever she is, told him that vortex would move and shift and that the spirit was on one point of the triangle. When the vortex shifts, the spirit moves with it."

Richard relays this bit of information objectively and without a hint of sarcasm. He then offers his own ideas about the realm of ghosts and spirits and other mysterious things: "I believe people—souls—who are trapped on this plane are innocent poltergeists that move things around. Angelic messengers are spirits that appear at crucial times in one's life to help someone." For clarification he adds, "Angels are the messengers of God in the Catholic church. Finally," Mr. Lindsley says, "there are the Fallen Angels. These are demonic. They want to mess up lives and destroy any chance of happiness. They do this with half-truths and lies and they bring only heartache. They are like a trickster."

More visitors enter the gift shop. I close my notebook and tell Richard that I'd like to look around the chapel. He takes my dollar admission and I enter just as another party is leaving. I step through the doorway and gasp. It's as if there is an enormous gravity—a critical mass of human experience—accumulated in the space that is so palpable it quite literally takes my breath away and raises the hair on the back of my neck.

Long beams of late afternoon sunlight slant from the small windows near the ceiling and haunting strains of Gregorian chants reverberate off massive white-washed adobe walls that have been mute witness to bloodshed and chaos, exuberant celebration, and solemn ceremony. I walk slowly up to the altar. The stunning altar screen is dominated by a winged St. Michael and flanked by Saint Terisa of Avila on the left and Saint Gertrude

San Miguel Mission altar screen.

the Great on the right. The old wood floors creak loudly with each step.

Suddenly, I turn to look up at the choir loft, to perhaps catch a fleeting glance of a man in black. But I see only bulky shapes that must be the ductwork of a modern heating system. At the altar rail, I see there are windows in the floor of the raised altar that show the original dirt floor and elevation of the church. On my left dozens of votive candles flicker, testament that this is still a sacred place of worship where mass is still said every Sunday. I sit down on one of the pews and soak in the majesty and mystery and continue to feel that prevailing, almost oppressive gravity of being in a place that has accumulated so much emotional energy. I admire the venerable old beams deeply incised with intricate carving and ponder the ominous implications of plastered over windows at the top of the north wall.

When other people enter the chapel giggling, I scowl at them for their irreverence and slip back into the gift shop. I thank Richard for the generosity of sharing his profound stories. He encourages me to contact Brother Lester, the chapel curator, for more stories. Before I leave, he hands me a brochure on the chapel that he wrote. He turns to the back page and taps it, saying, "This is important...you should use it in your book."

From the San Miguel brochure:

"In 1955, the Christian Brothers, who still own San Miguel Mission, commissioned an archeological study of the ancient chapel. This investigation revealed the original dirt floor and sanctuary steps, which can be seen just beyond the communion rail through openings in the sanctuary floor. During this dig, many human remains were found, estimated at three hundred people, most of whom are believed to be the devout Tlaxcalan Indians. The deceased or their families often made arrangements in those days to be interred if possible under the floor of a Catholic Church in the hope of being remembered in the prayers of the faithful who attended Mass there.

Today the Holy Sacrifice of the Mass is celebrated every Sunday at San Miguel Mission, and no doubt there are many of the living and deceased who are grateful. With its rich and ancient history, San Miguel Mission is often said to be haunted by countless spirits who are as diverse as those who worshiped and died there. Some visitors over the years have seen orbs of light dancing through the interior, while other guests have seen a women [sic] dressed all in white, kneeling in tears at the foot of the altar. Some have claimed to see a tall priest, dressed in a black cassock. On two occasions, people have seen six Indians emerging from the side hall, walking together across the front of the chapel. Finally, it has been reported by still other witnesses that they have seen young children running up and down the main aisle, singing songs and laughing with delight as only children can, spirit or not."

††††††††††††††

I meet with Brother Lester Lewis on another visit to San Miguel. The gift shop clerk directs me to a door at the far end of the gift shop. I walk through door into a hallway that leads to the front of the church. Across from me is another doorway, presumably to Brother Lester's office. When I step in the hallway, I get a decidedly uncomfortable feeling. Maybe it's the confusion about the exact location of Brother Lester's office, maybe it's because I'm suddenly nervous about meeting with Brother Lester, who, on the phone, has a very deep, authoritative voice. However, when I enter Brother Lester's office, the feeling vanishes. He welcomes me and gestures to a seat. With his deep voice, black cassock, and white two-lobed tie characteristic of the La Salle Christian brothers, he is a very commanding presence. But there is great kindness in his eyes and genuine warmth of personality. Before I can say anything beyond a greeting, he abruptly asks, "Are you psychic or clairvoyant?"

Brother Lester Lewis, curator of San Miguel Chapel. Brother Lester has heard many stories about paranormal occurrences during his tenure at San Miguel.

I stammer, not sure how to answer, and finally tell him that I always think those labels mean a person can summon such abilities at will and, while I have had paranormal experiences, they are not anything I ever planned or sought. He smiles and says, "Well, I think such things are more likely in women." Then he adds, "That's why I asked. Many women, whether they consider themselves psychic or not, when they enter San Miguel for the first time, it takes their breath away. This is something I've noticed. It literally takes their breath away."

I smile and tell him that's *exactly* what happened to me on my first visit when I stepped from the gift shop into the church. Then I explain my theory that it's the gravity of hundreds of years of intense emotional experience that has a breathtaking impact on the psyche.

Brother Lester begins the story of San Miguel with an intriguing statement: "Before the time of the Spanish, between 1200 and 1435, it was an Indian holy ground. Perhaps light came from the earth here the way it is said to have at Chimayo."

Chimayo, north of Santa Fe, is the location of a legendary shrine—the *Santuario de Chimayo*—built on a site the Native Tewa people described as a power spot, where there was a spring with healing properties. Brother Lester's mention of "light coming from the ground" referred to the story of a monk, Bernardo Abeyta, a Catholic missionary who saw a light coming from the ground near the Tewa power spot. The legend says he dug on the spot until his hands were bloody and eventually dug up an old wooden cross carved with the image of *"Our Lord of Esquipulas,"* the Black Christ renowned throughout Guatemala. He took the cross to a church in nearby Santa Cruz, but it immediately disappeared. He returned to the place where he found it and it was back in the hole. He retrieved the cross and returned it to the church, but it returned to the hole. After three occurrences of this mysterious event, a priest petitioned the Catholic hierarchy to erect a chapel at the site of the buried cross. That chapel became the *Santuario de Chimayo.*

After the chapel was built, Friar Abeyta fell seriously ill, and believing he was dying, sought to visit the *Santuario* one last time. As the legend goes, he walked the short distance and, when he neared the *Santuario,* he recognized the figure of the Black Christ in the doorway, but as he got closer, the apparition disappeared. Abeyta collapsed on the ground, but felt his strength returning. He recovered from his illness.

Today, the *Santuario de Chimayo* is the terminus of many pilgrimages, particularly for seekers of health miracles. Sand from a dinner plate-sized hole in the ground in the *Santuario* is praised for its healing properties and the small chapel is decorated with the discarded crutches and wheel chairs of those claimed to have been cured of their afflictions. Because so much dirt is taken from the hole, it is regularly replaced with clean dirt stored in a nearby shed.

Brother Lester makes a fascinating comment about the location of both the *Santuario de Chimayo* and San Miguel: "The Spanish learned that the way to overcome the Native people was to build on top of their holy sites."

He goes on to add, "There is a vortex of energy in San Miguel. It doesn't affect me...I can't feel it. I believe I am too close to it to experience it." He doesn't mention the psychic that Richard Lindsley noted, but speaks of the vortex as being a powerful force that affects only certain people.

Then he tells me about an Australian woman who came to the chapel to apply for a job as a clerk. "It was in 2002. She had extensive experience with indigenous people in Australia and had come to New Mexico to work with a Navajo shaman. After the interview I asked her if she'd like to see the chapel. As soon as she entered, she became very distressed and agitated and had to leave immediately. She explained that for eight years she had a disturbing recurring dream of small children crying in anguish. When she walked into the chapel, she recognized it from her dream. She worked at the gift shop for two years, but could not go into the chapel without feeling extreme distress. She described it as 'When I walked in, it was like a huge burden was placed on me.'"

Brother Lester goes on to describe an incident that happened in 2005. "An elderly woman and her husband were sitting in the pews reading the history of the chapel. A CD of Native American music was playing on the sound system. The woman saw six Indians in native dress walk down the hallway and examine the speakers. The woman went into the gift shop and remarked to the clerk that it was wonderful to see Indians in native dress come into the church and she asked if it happened often, if it was something like a reenactment the chapel performed. The clerk told her that, no, Indians never came into the church in native dress. The woman hurried back into the church and hustled her husband out. "My own community makes fun of that one," Brother Lester says with a rueful sigh, adding, "I get a lot of ribbing about that one."

Brother Lester tells me about a variety of small, fleeting incidents that various people have reported to him: *A human form rising up along the north wall stayed briefly near the ceiling and then disappeared...A shadowy form in black robes...Orbs of light floating in near the choir loft*.

In contrast to the Australian woman's vision of wailing, tormented children, a psychic reported to Brother Lester that she saw happy children running in the aisles much like the way she had seen them running and laughing in the aisles of churches in Central America. However, this psychic found the hallway leading to the front of the church very disturbing. That would be the same hallway that gave me a creepy feeling when I entered it. I remarked to Brother Lester that the hallway made me feel uncomfortable too and he smiled and nodded knowingly.

I ask Brother Lester about the Pueblo Revolt and if he believes that the death of so many people in one place contributes to the strange energy in San Miguel. He tells me two legends about Po'pay that I have not heard; that a Spanish boy allowed into the kiva when Po'pay was planning the revolt said that Po'pay's eyes turned red and glowed. Brother Lester comments that perhaps the red glowing eyes meant demonic possession. However, he also adds, "Po'pay *was* beaten in the Public Square." Another story Brother Lester recounted is that after the Indians had burned the church and driven out the last remaining Spaniards, Po'pay gathered up all the church articles that the friars were unable to carry, dressed up in a bishop's mitre, and carrying a chalice, led all his warriors down to the river to wash off their baptisms with soap made from yucca root.

Moving on from the serious topic of the Pueblo Revolt, Brother Lester remarks that there are also instances of a playful spirit believed to be a French priest who once lived in a residence in the area that is now the gift shop. The priest died there in 1950. He said the priest was noted for his sense of humor and playful pranks particularly on young girls. On one especially busy day at the gift shop, Brother Lester recalls, one of the three clerks started to sit down on the stool behind the cash register. Just as she did, and in full view of the other two clerks, the stool suddenly slid away and slammed into the wall. Brother Lester hurried in to investigate the commotion and told the young clerk, who was so distressed by the incident that she was ready to leave on the spot, "It's because he's French. It was just a playful prank."

Brother Lester's discussion turns to the large number of people buried under the floor of the church, around the church, even in the walls of the church, and the problem of constantly turning up human remains that must be forensically evaluated before being laid to rest in other places. He said that an archeological survey in 1955 determined that there were three hundred people buried in and around the church—all facing west. In 2005, during a construction of a path between San Miguel and the nearby Lamy building, the remains of a young Native American woman were found in the wall of the church. Skulls were found in the south wall.

At that point Brother Lester opens a drawer in his desk and takes out a small object. He remarks that a young boy who was fascinated by the window in the floor of the altar that shows the old part of the church begged Brother Lester to allow him to crawl under there. "So I let him because he was so interested. And this is what he found." Brother Lester hands me the small object. As the child of archeologists and an anthropology major, I immediately recognize it is part of a child's vertebrae. It is very yellow and there are tiny fissures and cracks filled with dirt. I turn it over in my hand, incredulous. What amazes me is how heavy it feels for its size. I remark on this to Brother Lester and he agrees that it *does* feel uncommonly heavy for something so small. As I hold the bone, it occurs to me that it is as if San Miguel is telling stories of its past with both strange events and physical evidence. The earth continues to push up fragments of the past the way frost heave pushes up stones in a field. Brother Lester remarks that other times human remains have been inadvertently uncovered, elders of nearby pueblos are consulted to determine if the remains should be reburied on native land as mandated by the Native American Grave Protection and Repatriation Act of 1990. However, the Native people don't claim the remains because they are Tlaxcalan.

Before I leave, Brother Lester offers to take me on a tour of San Miguel. While it doesn't take my breath away to enter the second time, it is still a very solemn and inspiring space. We pause in front of the mysterious painting of a shadowy figure meeting a dark-haired woman on a stormy night. A church looms in the background. Brother Lester explains that some people object to the painting because it is so dark and mysterious, inferring that it is sinister but he said he believes it is about redemption.

5

THE OLDEST HOUSE

La Casa Vieja de Analco (The Oldest House).

I ts accurate and formal name is La Casa Vieja de Analco. However, the two-story adobe building on East de Vargas Street is usually just called "The Oldest House." The brochure about it sub-titles it, The Oldest House in the U.S.A. The structure called "The Oldest House" is actually built on top of an even older house, an ancient Native American pueblo that was part of the village on which both the Oldest House and San Miguel Mission were built. More accurately, it could be described as: "The Oldest House of European Origin that is Known in North America Until a Viking Long House is Found Somewhere Else that Causes a Huge Archeological Controversy." Irreverence for the designation "Oldest" aside, the Oldest House, like San Miguel directly to the south across narrow de Vargas Street, has a profound gravity of accumulated human experience—and that human experience survives as fascinating stories, both *supernatural* and historical.

Tlaxcalan servants constructed the Oldest House at the same time they built San Miguel Mission, sometime between 1598 and 1610. Its original purpose was to house the Franciscan Friars and Brothers. During the Pueblo Revolt of 1680, it was captured and occupied by the rebelling pueblo people.

One of the more interesting stories about the Oldest House relates to the occupancy of a pair of brujas, the Spanish word for female witches. Accounts of the brujas living in the Oldest House vary from the very late 1600s and early 1700s to the early 1800s. Most stories, as well as Brother Lester, corroborate the seventeenth century time frame. Unlike European witches of Celtic and Teutonic heritage who did not—contrary to popular belief—practice magic with ill intent or to cause harm or manipulation of will, brujas and brujos (male witches) in the Americas were known to practice "black magic." According to Brother Lester, the brujas who lived in the Oldest House were said to throw fireballs at San Miguel Mission because they did not like the Church.

About the same time the Santa Fe brujas were being verbally vilified, Salem, Massachusetts residents were actually hanging women accused of witchcraft. However, the Santa Fe brujas never feared for their lives because many residents, while publicly condemning the brujas, clandestinely visited them to buy remedies, herbs, love potions, or to have the brujas cast spells for them.

Such was the case of Juan Espinoza. The young Spaniard sought out the brujas because he wanted to win the favor of a beautiful woman and decided the easiest way to accomplish that was to have the brujas mix up a love potion. The entrepreneurial brujas would guarantee the results of their work if they were paid in gold. Unfortunately, none of Juan Espinoza's efforts, the love potion or subsequent booster spells cast by the brujas, influenced the fair lady and she married another.

Juan Espinoza demanded a refund of his gold from the brujas because they had guaranteed their work. But the brujas refused to return his gold. In keeping with the tradition of the time, when there were no courts or tort claims for non-performance of a guaranteed spell, Juan did what dashing young men were said to do: He drew his sword. Lunging menacingly at the brujas, Juan was perhaps as inept at swordsmanship as he had been at courting beautiful women. One of the brujas stuck out her foot and tripped him. Juan fell to floor, the sword slipped from his hand, and, in a classic one-two maneuver, the other bruja grabbed the sword and lopped off Juan's head.

The brujas were charged with murder. However, the governor—said to be under the spell of the brujas (one that apparently worked)—dismissed the case and neither woman was ever tried. According to legend, the brujas preserved Juan's body and kept it at the house as a warning to others who might ask for a refund on services rendered. When the brujas left, the remains of Juan Espinosa disappeared with them.

The legend continues that, on the anniversary of his death, Juan's head rolls down de Vargas Street as if bowled out of the hands of a bruja. Further embellishments of the story say that Juan Espinoza is the headless horseman who rides down Alto Street brandishing his sword. However, other versions of the headless horseman legend identify him as a cowboy.

The Oldest House has been at various times a residence, a curio shop, gift shop, and museum of Spanish colonial and pioneer New Mexico artifacts. A number of accounts of the history of the Oldest House related that one of the more macabre "attractions" was a mummified Native American man named

"Geronimi" that sat in a rocking chair in the far corner of one of the rooms with one hand extended as if begging. According to the stories, "Geronimi" lived in the area near the Oldest House and slept in a hollowed out place in the ground. When he didn't show up at the mission, the Brothers began to look for him and found him dead in the Oldest House. Inexplicably, he was left there to mummify and was put on exhibit. He was removed from the Oldest House in 1995 to be put on display in another location. Some visitors claim to still see his presence in the place where he used to sit.

Many people claim to feel very uncomfortable in the Oldest House. According to Brother Lester, psychics have variously identified "a hostile" and "fearsome" presence while yet another psychic identified it more as a guardian presence. Brother Lester said that because of the strong feelings of evil that some visitors experience there has been a cleansing performed and he has also personally blessed the building.

I figured if any spirit had a reason to be angry and disruptive, it would seem to be Geronimi for having his earthly remains displayed in such a disrespectful manner. I questioned Brother Lester about the appalling tourist attraction of a begging mummy and he laughed loudly. "I wondered that same thing. I wanted to find out everything I could about him when I first got here. There was a Brother here who was ninety years old and I asked him 'Brother, what is the story of the mummy?' And *he* laughed. He told me that there *was* an old Indian man who lived in the Oldest House in the 1920s. He hollowed out a place in the dirt floor and that's where he slept. He did odd jobs for the Brothers. The Indian had an old enamel coffee pot and he would come to the Brothers at the mission with the coffee pot. The Brothers would offer him a plate of food, but he didn't want to eat off a plate—he wanted all the food put in the coffee pot. He would take the coffee pot full of food back to the Oldest House to eat. He didn't die in the Oldest House; he died in a cornfield. And it wasn't a mummy. It was a medical model."

Seeing the look of relief on my face, Brother Lester laughs. "Well it was so real. It was real to me! And Brother thought that was funny too, that I thought it was real. Brother told me that the people who had the curio shop in the Oldest House in the early 1950s heard the story of the old Indian and decided to create a tourist attraction by dressing up this medical model of a mummy as an Indian." Brother Lester demonstrates how the "mummy" sat, not with his hand outstretched as the stories I had read, but with them resting, palms up, in his lap. "People did throw money at him though," Brother Lester says, "I would find all kinds of money on the floor around him."

It's another example of a seed of truth grown into a grandiose tale.

On a more mysterious and mischievous note, Brother Lester remarked on a strange incident that took place a number of years ago. The gift shop proprietor had a small Christmas tree in the shop during the holiday season. Each night she would unplug the tree before she left and each morning the tree would be plugged in and lit when she opened.

Today, the main gift shop area of the Oldest House is large and well-lit however, the western wing is like a warren of interconnected rooms that we in New Mexico sometimes refer to as a "rifle house." That is, rooms are added one next to the other with no hallways so that you could fire a rifle from one end to the other through the doorways and not hit anything. The walls are thick and the doorways between rooms, narrow and misshapen. Perhaps the creepy feeling people get is from the massiveness of the adobe walls and the ominous way light slants in through the tiny, dusty deep-set windows.

The back rooms are filled with historic relics characteristic of New Mexico's Spanish colonial heritage. In one room a coffin of the old style trapezoid shape sits in front of a small window. Above the coffin is the legend of Juan Espinoza in a simple frame. When I visit, the coffin is closed, but Brother Lester tells me there is a

Window in the Oldest House.

The mock coffin of Juan Epinoza features a plaque telling the story.

headless medical skeleton in it. He relates that the arrival of the bogus Juan Espinoza was heralded by a mock funeral procession down de Vargas Street with the new gift shop proprietress swinging an incense censer and Brother Lester joining the procession in simulated solemnity. "I'm surprised I didn't get censored for that," he laughs.

Besides the old coffin, the museum is filled with colonial and pioneer artifacts resting against the walls as if they were just put down by ancient hands. There are two hand-made cradles that attest to the toughness of the early Santa Fe residents—even infants. One is made from a scooped out cottonwood log and hung by thongs from the ceiling; the other is rectangular and made with no glue or nails. A rattle made of bear-claws hangs from the top of it.

The ceiling of the Oldest House is the traditional viga–log support–and latilla–small closely placed sticks. Plant material hangs through the latillas, making the ceiling look particularly authentic and, some might think, creepy.

A pioneer display in the Oldest house.

On my first visit to the Oldest House I talk with clerk Jackie Pacheco, a Santa Fe native and member of one of Santa Fe's oldest families for whom Pacheco Street is named. I ask her about strange energy or weird things happenings. Contrary to all the stories of bad or angry energy and feeling uncomfortable, Jackie smiles and proclaims, "I love it here. I love this place. For me it is very peaceful." As far as strange activities, she said nothing has ever really happened. She remarked how her father used to tell her stories that young boys would dare each other to run down de Vargas Street between San Miguel and the Oldest House "because it really could be a scary place at night." No doubt because of the stories of heads bowled by brujas.

The only incident that she could recall in her tenure at the shop happened on "a strange day." She said, "It was just one of those strange days, I can't really describe it. We had a cat in the shop then and the cat was just going nuts and acting weird. Then this handsome guy came in. He said, 'I'm Juan Espinoza.'" Jackie and I concur that it is not an uncommon name in New Mexico, but then she adds, "but the strange thing was just his attitude. He said, 'I'm that guy in the story. I'm Juan Espinoza.'" Jackie said that he even took out his driver's license to show her that was his name. She said there was just something weird and strange about the whole encounter.

On another visit I talked with current leaseholder, Suzanne Alba. I knew she'd have some interesting stories because when I talked to her about an interview on the phone she said, "I didn't believe in ghosts, but I do now!"

Suzanne tells me that when she first acquired the shop it had been closed for about five years and was in significant disrepair. She said her initial reaction to the place was that it was creepy. Plus, there were the stories of ghosts. She said her husband "really had to convince me that I could make it into a nice shop. He said the ghost stuff was silly."

Suzanne tells me the first event happened right away, when she and her husband were fixing up the shop.

"We were here one day working on the shop and our son Emory who must have been about nine at the time was playing around inside and out back. My husband, Christopher, is an architect and a contractor and he was building this display case." Suzanne walks over to a glass-topped display case near the front door and demonstrates how he was slightly crouched down. "The front door was closed tight. All of a sudden it just started to open. But not open like it was blown open by a wind, it opened kind of slowly, the way it would open if somebody opened it. Then it just slammed shut. I said, 'Christopher, did you just see the door open?' He said, 'Yeah, it was Emory coming in,' and I said, 'No, Emory is over there.'" Suzanne pointed to the back of the shop where their son was playing.

"We both kind of looked at each other and Christopher said, 'Well, *that* was weird. Maybe there is something to this ghost stuff.'"

Suzanne leads me to the back of the shop where a wall is painted a startlingly bright shade of pink. There is an old door in the center of the wall with a tiny metal sign "Personnel Only." "The next thing that happened was scary. I was closing up and I was by myself. It was December so it gets dark around five o'clock. I had turned off all the lights except for the Christmas tree so I'd have a little bit of light." She points to a small tree on a table used to display handcrafted ornaments year-round. She opens the door and shows me how the cord goes under the door and plugs into a socket about five feet up on the wall outside a tiny bathroom. "I went into the bathroom and shut the door. The next thing I hear is the cord being pulled out of the socket. I opened the door and it was pitch black. I didn't know if somebody was in there or what had happened, but I was scared and I started to call out, 'Christopher! Brother Lester!'" Suzanne demonstrates how the cord makes a distinct sound when it is pulled from the socket. "See, it's not like it fell out. It was pulled."

Suzanne said that incident really rattled her and that she started researching ghosts on the Internet. "They really can actually move physical things, I discovered. There was a story of a woman who was shoved from behind. That terrified me. I didn't want to come back. Brother Lester guessed that maybe the remodeling had kind of stirred things up. He said, 'It's those darn ghosts.' It took a lot for me to come back."

Stirred up ghosts presented another problem for Suzanne as a merchant: Nocturnal trips to the Oldest House because the alarm system was tripped by movement, primarily in the back two rooms. "You can ask the alarm company about their log for this zone, for nighttime calls because of movement inside buildings. It's off the charts."

She went on to describe one particularly disturbing incident when she came to check out the Oldest House in response to notification from the alarm company. "Since I had to go by myself, I took my very fierce dog with me. We got to the door. I unlocked and opened it. My dog braced himself against the door jam with his front paws and absolutely refused to enter. I tried to drag him, but he sensed something was wrong and was totally terrified. He just dug in and refused to budge. I finally had to take him back to the car. I've never seen him act like that. So much for my very fierce dog."

"I wasn't the only one having troubles around here," Suzanne continues. "The previous owner of the little shop across the street was really having problems with her business and she suspected that it might be because a ghost was making customers feel uncomfortable. People would come in and turn around and leave. Finally, it got to the point that she started talking to the ghost. As soon as she opened up in the morning, she would ask the ghost to go hang out at the church [San Miguel] for the day and that it could come back at night. The really weird thing is *that* seemed to work. Business picked up."

"There are just so many stories," Suzanne says, taking a deep breath. "I'm trying to remember them all. Oh, yeah. A woman came into the store, a psychic type. She said, 'Do you know you have a ghost?'" Suzanne laughs. "By then it was kind of funny. *Of course I knew I had a ghost.* So I said, yes. The woman asked me if I could see it and I said no. She told me that she could see him and he was standing behind me. She told me he was old. Not old as in age, but from a very early time. He was wearing a loincloth. She told me he was a protector of this place...that he watched over the store. And you know," Suzanne says, pausing to rap her knuckles on the wood of a display case, "I haven't had the kinds of problems with theft that so many of the other shops in Santa Fe have had."

"Let's see, what else?" Suzanne wonders. "You've heard the story of the brujas throwing fireballs haven't you?" I reply that I have. She points to a large picture leaning up against a display case of a large old adobe house with a smaller ruin next to it. "That's where my mother grew up in Black Mesa [north of Santa Fe]." She points to the smaller house. "It's almost dissolved down to the ground now. My mother used to tell me that brujas traveled up the river in fireballs and that they would see these fireballs going up the river every once in awhile."

"Oh yeah, the best story of all," Suzanne says suddenly. "At least I think it's the best and most remarkable."

She tells me that one day a very old and frail man came into the shop with his great-grandson. "I think he said he was 96. He told me he used to live in this part," she says gesturing to the gift shop area, "and that they charged a nickel for people to look at the Oldest House part. His father was a janitor at the college and his mother was a housekeeper. He said his family was very poor and that when his younger brother fell and hit his head and was seriously injured they didn't have money for the doctor. Apparently, some large growth formed where he hit his head. A doctor from the Mayo Clinic happened to see his little brother when they were playing out here in front. The doctor spoke to the parents and told them how important it was to have this growth attended to. The old man said that his parents explained to the doctor that they didn't have any money. So this doctor says he would take care of it and pay for everything. He said that the doctor had the younger brother flown to…where is the Mayo Clinic?

"Rochester, Minnesota?" I offer.

"Yeah, something like that. Back when there was only one Mayo Clinic. Anyway, the little brother came back and everything was fine for about a year. Then, the old man said that the growth or whatever it was started to come back. One day when he was watching after his little brother while his parents were at work the little brother said, 'Get mom!' The old man said that they didn't have a phone and that his little brother was very agitated, that something was wrong and he needed his mom. He said he made the decision to run to the college and try to find his father because the college was closer than where his mother worked. He brought his father back."

Suzanne pauses and seems to get a little emotional.

"By then, the old man is almost crying. He says that when he got back with his dad his little brother was on the verge of death and was still asking for his mother. And then he died. Right here. Suzanne points toward the front of the gift shop."

We are both quiet and I continue to scribble in my notebook.

"I really felt like, for some reason, he had to come back here and tell that story," Suzanne says. "He was so old and frail and his great-grandson was helping him get around, but it seemed so important for him come here and to tell me. I wonder if the spirit of the little boy is here too. Maybe that was the thing with the door."

I agree it is a very remarkable story and strange that the man would show up just to tell it and then leave.

"Another thing that was weird," Suzanne says, "and I don't know if it's ghost-related, but there is just absolutely no way to explain it. I came in one morning and the shop was filled with pigeons. Pigeons! They were flying everywhere and I couldn't figure out how they got in."

Gesturing, she says, "Come here and take a look at this." She points to a small area in the ceiling between the newer part of the building that is the gift shop and the actual Oldest House part that is the little museum. "There was a hole there. I have no idea how it got there, but apparently the pigeons got into the upstairs part and then somehow made a hole and got in. But what was really amazing, after I got them all shooed out is that, looking from the outside at the windows, there were all these beautiful marks on the glass that looked like imprints of little angels. I guess they were imprints of where they flew into the windows trying to escape."

As we're standing in the junction between the gift shop and the Oldest House museum, Suzanne remarks, "I would say that one out of thirty people who come in here start to come into this part, and then they immediately leave—they pop out like corks. I ask them if they felt uncomfortable and they say yes or they don't say anything and just leave. We had the place blessed and things were better for awhile, but now it seems like it's kind of back. In this part, it just feels like something oppressive, something pushing down on your shoulders. I don't like to come back here."

I also visit the building directly across the street from San Miguel, the one where the former proprietor issued morning ghost relocation orders. When I approach the door, I see it's propped open about a foot with a wedge to keep it from closing. I push on it to open it further, but when I do, it feels like the door has bumped into someone standing on the other side. I pause, to give them time to step aside, and then I push more gently and peer around the door—and find nobody there. I push the door more firmly and the proprietress of the shop, phone in hand, steps over from the other side of the shop to pull the door completely open. It was a strange little experience, and one that if it had happened any place else, would not have provoked a 'hmm, kind of odd.' But it's a place supposedly imbued with weirdness and part of an "Energy Vortex" — even the oddest little thing can take on otherworldly implications.

I wander around trying to get any kind of feel or try to find what pushed back when I opened the door. Like the Oldest House, it is a collection of rooms stuck together in a warren-like arrangement as expansion dictated. I wanted to talk to the shopkeeper, but she is deeply engrossed in her phone conversation. Finally, she calls out, "Can I help you?" I tell her that I'm a writer looking for ghosts and I wondered if she'd had any unusual experiences. She covers the phone with her palm and says, "Not really. I haven't had the place that long. There was this one thing though, right when we were first moving in. We came in one morning and this glass shelf had fallen to the floor and shattered in a million pieces. I have no idea how that could have possibly happened."

"Thanks," I say.

She returns to her phone conversation and I feel like I am interrupting her so I leave. As I approach the heavy wooden door I look to see if there is something on the floor, something on the wall, anything that could possible explain how it distinctly felt like I was bumping it into a person. There is nothing there.

LA POSADA
& THE MYSTERIOUS
JULIA STAAB

An exterior view of La Posada with the Raven holding a Pear sculpture.

J ulia Staab is, unquestionably, Santa Fe's most famous ghost. "Google" her on the Internet—and there are tens of thousands of hits about her plus hundreds of stories.

She has been the subject of an "Unsolved Mysteries" episode, as well as an episode of "Weird Stories." Most accounts of Julia's life begin with information from the New Mexico Tourism Department's website.

"Amassing a fortune as a major supply contractor for the U.S. Army during the Civil War, Abraham Staab built the beautiful three-story brick mansion for his wife Julia. Constructed in the French Second Empire-style, the residence was decorated with the finest European materials and furnishings. The large Staab family, including six children, lived primarily on the second floor, which was accessed by a grand staircase. On the third floor was a beautiful ballroom that soon became one of the social entertainment centers of Santa Fe society, as Julia loved to show off the home that she adored.

"After the death of her seventh child, a son, soon after birth, Julia fell into a deep depression and her hair was said to have turned prematurely white. Julia had several more unsuccessful pregnancies and eventually took to her room, where she spent almost all of her time until her death at the age of 52 in 1896. Rumors at the time persisted that in Julia's later years, she had gone completely crazy."

Besides this rather benign overview of her life, there are other darker stories about Julia; that Abraham was a promiscuous, tyrannical husband who first regarded Julia as arm-candy, then a baby machine, and finally an embarrassment. Indeed, such an embarrassment he locked her away in her room. Some accounts say Abraham murdered Julia; other accounts merely hint that somehow he caused her death.

In all the stories, there seems to be agreement that in the beginning of her life with Abraham, Julia was the consummate gracious hostess and that she loved her home. Today there are no visible external remnants of the elegant brick mansion Abraham Staab had built with European materials imported with great difficulty via wagon train. First, a fire in the early 1900s destroyed the ballroom. Later, after Abraham's death, the Nason family purchased the house. They began remodeling it, adding adobe casitas around the sprawling six-acre compound and converting it to a hotel, La Posada (the inn).

Today, the Staab house has been completely *adobified*. That is, a heavy adobe and pseudo-adobe façade has consumed the entire Victorian brick structure so, from the outside, it looks like all the other pueblo-revival architectural style buildings in Santa Fe's historic district. Ironically, if Abraham Staab were to apply for a building permit in modern Santa Fe with plans for his brick Victorian mansion, he would likely be denied because such a dwelling wouldn't pass contemporary Santa Fe's strict zoning restrictions on height and style enacted to preserve the city's historic look.

Guests at the La Posada, now part of the Rock Resort chain of elegant hotels, report bizarre occurrences, such as trash cans sliding across the floors, and more than one ghost tour participant has reported seeing a fleeting image in the mirror in what is supposed to be Julia's room. Some even claim to have pictures of the image in the mirror. Julia is said to have caused havoc during a variety of remodeling projects and to have wrecked video equipment of a group trying to capture some indication of her presence. There are numerous reports of the..."*feeling of being watched," "a sudden coldness," an "enveloping chill," and a tinkling chandelier that "can't possibly be affected by breezes or air currents.*"

According to a press release from Rock Resorts, the current owners of La Posada, "Julia's old bedroom, now the hotel's Room 100, is called the Julia Staab Suite, and many hotel guests, hotel staff, and local residents have seen her ghost and felt her presence. One hotel guest even saw her face reflected in the mirror while he was shaving!"

Those who claim to have seen Julia's visage describe a "translucent" woman with prematurely gray hair and "intense eyes" in nineteenth century dress. As with many ghosts inhabiting hotels or restaurants, there are reports of floating glasses that then fall to the floor and other disruptions related to dishes and utensils. Wait staff blame her for knocking trays off their hands.

There are also several isolated incidents involving a male presence. In one case a security guard heard a man talking loudly in a lounge area, but when he opened the door there was nobody there. In another instance a female guest reported a man in a waistcoat standing over her bed.

A night auditor who liked to nap on a couch awakened one night, astonished to discover he was completely naked, covered by a blanket, with his clothes folded neatly at the end of the couch.

In contrast to the stories of disruptive disturbances, some La Posada employees have had experiences with a very benevolent presence. One La Posada employee called her "the hostess with the mostest" and said she reminds him to always give the best possible service to guests. There is a particularly mysterious and endearing story of Julia's concern for the comfort of guests at La Posada; a story that seems much more in character with her real life persona.

One autumn evening the La Posada suddenly got very cold. In the high desert mountains the temperature can plummet when a cold front moves in, sometimes twenty degrees or more in an hour. The person in charge of turning on the heat in La Posada was on vacation or somehow unavailable, so hotel personnel scrambled to provide extra blankets and portable heaters to chilled guests because nobody on staff knew how to start the furnace. The front desk clerk answered the phone and heard an irate female voice say, "My guests are cold!" Click. Within the hour the heat came on and flowed through the La Posada and nobody on staff knew how it happened. Also more in character with her gracious hospitality are the mysterious filling bathtubs as if Julia is drawing baths for guests.

A former La Posada employee and life-long Santa Fe resident, Gloria, told me she was very familiar with the stories of Julia when she applied for a job at La Posada. As Gloria sat waiting for her interview, she said she rather flippantly thought, 'Julia, if you want me to work here, give me a sign.' "I was just kind of joking around, kind of mocking," Gloria said, "but then the lights started flashing. Not just a little bit, but on, off, on, off. When the guy came to interview me, he said, 'Let's move to another room. There must be something wrong with the wiring. It's an old building you know.' Yeah, I knew. But it seemed like a sign to me."

Gloria goes on to tell me that one of the other women working there was going around turning off lights for the evening. She walked into the Rose Room, a room supposedly dedicated to Julia, and saw a shadow of a woman, but there was no physical person casting the shadow.

There was another time when Gloria believes Julia tried to communicate with her. "I had this very strong urgency to go up to Julia's room. I don't know why, I just did. The bed faces the window in there. Somebody had placed Archangel Michael candles in an arc around the front of the bed. Maybe Julia thought it was dangerous to leave so many candles burning. Maybe that's why I had the strong feeling to go up there, to blow the candles out. So I did."

I visited the elegant and beautifully appointed La Posada and settled into a comfortable couch in a nook in the lobby, hoping to talk to someone about Julia and to get a feel for her beloved home. The lobby of La Posada is traditional adobe architecture with plaster walls, beams, and a latilla ceiling. A fire crackles in the fireplace—something that is said to happen spontaneously on occasion and is attributed to Julia. Two ornate brass mirrors adorn the top of the fireplace. I wonder what Julia would think of the art in the lobby nook: two enormous early eighteenth century Peruvian paintings of Archangels Michael and Gabriel, presiding menacingly from opposite walls.

Doorway to the Staab House portion of La Posada.

Across the lobby is a door to a long staircase, down which the visage of Julia is said to sometimes float. A small sign next to the doorway marks it as "Staab House." There are rooms off of the lobby that retain the Victorian styling as does the bar, Fuego, where she is supposed to have floated glasses off the shelf one-by-one, crashing them to the floor. Since Fuego means fire in Spanish, one can't help but wonder, since Julia's beloved ballroom was destroyed by fire, if she might not be irritated that the bar would be dubbed fire.

As I sat in La Posada's lobby, I suddenly felt an intense curiosity to find out the real story of Julia Staab. It bothered me that there were so many contradictions in the stories I had read about her life. Indeed, even the authenticity of her portrait is in question. There are many pictures of it on the Internet and various tourist publications: Dressed in a formal white satin gown with puffy sleeves and seated on a chair in front of a vase of roses, a dark-haired woman stares with an almost bored expression, her hands loosely clasped in her lap, a strap, perhaps for a purse, is looped around her right wrist. There are claims that the woman is actually one of Julia's daughters or a niece since it was allegedly painted in 1939, nearly forty years after Julia died. As I continued sitting in the La Posada, the curiosity turned to a disturbed sense that Julia's life story hadn't been told with the accuracy or authenticity she wanted.

First there were the obvious contradictions in the account of the tragic death of her child that supposedly sent her over the edge. All accounts—and I'd read perhaps a dozen—documented that the child was a boy, and that it was Julia's seventh child, but accounts varied regarding the child's death from "right after birth" to "toddler."

There were accounts that attributed both the child's death, and later Julia's, to the hand of Abraham Staab. I decided to make another visit to Fairview Cemetery and find the Staab family plot. Perhaps that would provide information about the baby that figured so prominently in all the stories.

Monument over the graves of Abraham and Julia Staab.

Unlike the Umberhine graves, the Staab family plot was not difficult to find, being one of the most prominent in Fairview Cemetery. It is marked by a towering dark gray granite obelisk topped with a Greco-Roman urn with something resembling a chiseled marble cloth emerging from the top of the urn. The plot is surrounded by a pipe fence with an ornate rusty iron gate that gives off an eerie creak when opened. Julia (although the monument says "Julie") and her husband, Abraham, rest in the center of the plot, under the obelisk, flanked by four of their sons. Oddly the graves, closest to Abraham and Julia—Julius on the right and Paul on the left—have upright headstones. Next to Julius lies Edward and beside Paul rests Arthur, both under a flat headstone. The graves of Julia and Abraham are slightly elevated with a raised concrete curb around it. I was touched to see several clumps of tulips pushing up through cracks in the dry sand—everything that lives in the desert fights and struggles to survive. While the tulips will likely always be stunted and probably never flower because of lack of water, the fact that it was tulips rather than tumbleweeds emerging from the plot seemed almost miraculous.

And the infant son? In the far corner of the plot is a tiny wizened lilac bush as tall as the simple yellow marble headstone it seems to guard. The pitted marble is a stark contrast to the ornate polished granite headstones of other members of the Staab family. It marks the grave of an infant. An infant girl, Henriette, born July 22, 1883, died August 8, 1883. If the centerpiece of the story of Julia's alleged insanity was the death of her child, it seemed bizarre that not one single story had the sex of the child correct.

As I marveled at the tulips on Abraham and Julia's grave, it occurred to me that perhaps a family member planted and tended them. A family as prominent and as large as the Staabs surely had surviving members that could attest to, or debunk, the myriad versions of stories about Julia and Abraham.

I decided to consult *genealogy.com*. Plugging "Julia Staab, New Mexico" into the search function returned several hits. There

Staab family plot at Fairview Cemetery.

The grave of baby girl, Henriette Staab.

was information from a U.S. Western and Prairie States Census Index of 1880 that listed Abraham Staab, age 41. It indicated he was married and that his birthplace, and that of his parents, was Prussia. However, most intriguing was a link to a brief message board discussion with this tantalizing post:

> Posted by Robert Ach
> November 23, 2002
> "I am the great-great-grandson of Abraham Staab, who was born in Westphalia, Germany in 1839, emigrated to the US, and ended up in Santa Fe, New Mexico, where he became a very successful merchant. His house is still standing and is part of the La Posada Inn in Santa Fe. And yes, legend has it that his wife, Julia Staab, still haunts the house. I'd be very interested in talking to anyone who has interest in the New Mexico Staabs."

Well, I was interested in talking about the New Mexico Staabs—very interested. Since the email address for Mr. Ach was six years old, I felt like I was tossing out a cyber note in a bottle into the vastness of the Internet, so I made my message brief:

"I found a message you posted on Genealogy Forum—from way back in 2002— stating you were the great-great-grandson of Abraham Staab...If this email address still works, might I ask you some questions about your famous ancestors? I'm interested in the more personal stories not the sensationalist junk."

And Robert Ach replied.

In a subsequent email, I told Mr. Ach that I was seeking the "real" story of Abraham and Julia Staab, that somehow I had a feeling that what I'd been reading was inaccurate and sensationalized, and I felt compelled to tell a more accurate story. I noted that some accounts said that Abraham murdered Julia and I wondered about the accuracy of those reports.

I didn't hear back from Robert Ach for several days, but when he replied it was with a thoughtful, moving email that made sense of all the legends and lore. His story—*the real story*—is devoid of mayhem and murder and is actually more fascinating and poignant than all of the sensational tales. I could not improve on Mr. Ach's eloquence, sincerity, or facts so here is his account of the "real" story of Julia and Abraham Staab.

✝✝✝✝✝✝✝✝✝✝✝✝✝

Hi Susan,

Murdered! Ha, that's a new one. No, unfortunately, real life is much more mundane, and yet perhaps sadder.

Abraham Staab was born in Westphalia, Germany on February 27, 1839. He was Jewish, and in 1854, at the age of 15, he sailed for the U.S. seeking to escape military conscription, persecution, and life in the Jewish ghettos. He first went to Norfolk, Virginia, where he worked for relatives in the grocery business for $1 a week. Having gained some business experience, he came west to Santa Fe in 1858 with his brother Zadoc. They established a small retail store, and within two years it was the largest wholesale goods business in the whole Southwest. Staab was dealing in huge amounts of money by then, in days when there weren't any banks. He used to store the silver in his offices. He would lend money and extend credit to customers who needed it, and won a reputation for being absolutely fair and honest, which no doubt helped his business even more.

After becoming prosperous, Staab returned to Germany to find a bride. In 1865 he married Julia Schuster, one of eight sisters and two brothers, the children of Levi and Jette Schuster. They moved into an adobe house on Burro Alley, one block from the New Mexico Museum in Santa Fe. Julia bore eight children:

Anna, 1866-1936 (my great-grandmother, who married Louis Ilfeld, my great-grandfather); Delia, 1868-1951 (married Louis Baer); Bertha, 1871-1933 (married Max Nordhaus); Paul, 1872-1915; Arthur, 1873-1952; Julius, 1874-1913; Edward (Teddy), 1875-1968; and Henriette, 1883 (died in infancy)

Julia was never in very good health and was an invalid for most of her life in Santa Fe, supposedly due to difficulties encountered during her many pregnancies. It's clear that she also suffered from depression, which in those days, before Prozac and psychotherapy, was simply impossible to treat. One family account says that in 1892 she had a "dreadful accident" which the doctor ordered her daughters to report to their father. While there are no other details, I believe it's possible that this was a suicide attempt, although that's speculation on my part.

Whenever she became seriously ill, Julia would be sent to Germany where her sisters would nurse her back to health. Of course, this was a rough trip in those days, the worst part being the stagecoach ride along the Santa Fe Trail to Trinidad, Colorado, where the railroad east began. Along the trail the chances of encounters with bandits or worse were quite high. On one of her trips, the Archbishop Lamy, who was a friend of the Staab family, asked two nuns to accompany Julia in the stagecoach to Trinidad. One of the nuns, Sister Blandina Segale, described the events of that trip in a book called *At the End of the Santa Fe Trail* (an amusing book of Santa Fe history, which I recommend if you can find a copy). According to Sister Blandina, as the stagecoach was moving along the Trail, Billy the Kid and his gang rode up to rob the wagon train. Luckily, Sister Blandina had once nursed Billy back to health during an illness. When she saw him riding up, she stuck her head out of the stagecoach and waved. Seeing it was her, he smiled and waved back, and ordered his men to break off the attack. They then escorted the wagon train along the Trail—to make sure no one else robbed them!

In 1884 the Staabs built the three-story house that is now La Posada. Julia was a gracious hostess and a fixture of Santa Fe society, when her health permitted. Abraham Staab himself was one of the most noted citizens in town. He was one of the founders, and the first president of, the Santa Fe Chamber of Commerce. He was a director of the First National Bank of Santa Fe. He was also instrumental in working to defeat the attempted removal of the State Capital from Santa Fe to Albuquerque.

My favorite Abraham Staab story involves the building of the Santa Fe Cathedral. The story is that Abraham and several prominent citizens used to get together and play poker on Friday nights. Archbishop Lamy used to come by to watch and talk with the men, but of course never played cards himself. One night Lamy was looking quite dejected, and Staab asked him what was wrong. Lamy said that the building of the cathedral, which at that time was half-finished, would have to be stopped indefinitely because they had run out of money. Staab told him that was not a problem, that he would lend Lamy the money needed to finish the cathedral. Well, the cathedral got built, but then it became apparent that it was going to be impossible to raise the money to pay Staab back his loan. Upon learning this, Staab approached Lamy and told him to forget it, that the money was his gift and he did not need to be repaid (remember that Staab was Jewish, not Catholic). Lamy, in his gratitude, had the Jewish name for God, Yahweh, inscribed in Hebrew on the triangular keystone above the main entrance to the cathedral. And if you look at the keystone today, above the main entrance, you can see that the Hebrew inscription is still there, above the door to the Catholic cathedral.

Despite his civic mindedness, though, Abraham was also apparently in many ways a tyrant with his family. When his son Arthur married a gentile, Abraham had him disinherited, in spite of the fact that the rest of the family found the woman quite charming. His son Teddy became a doctor in Philadelphia, and was setting up his practice as a pediatrician, when Abraham ordered him to come home to take care of Julia.

There was other family tragedy as well. Their son Julius committed suicide, for unknown reasons (although this was years after Julia's death). Another son, Paul, was an epileptic due to a childhood illness and was an invalid for much of his life. And of course their last child, Henriette, a daughter, died shortly after birth. Eight years later, on May 15, 1896, Julia died. I do not know the circumstances of her death, but her terrible depression and ever-worsening health were undoubtedly the cause. I'm sure the death of her last child was a terrible blow, and I suspect that part of her continual depression was post-partum. Again, it so sad to think that diseases that are so treatable now, could cause so much suffering just one hundred years ago.

So there you have it. No murder, no crime—just a hard life and continual battles with illness and depression that finally took their inevitable toll.

Still, the three eldest daughters all married successful businessmen and went on to have happy prosperous families. Teddy lived until 1968, and apparently was quite a character (he never married and was obviously gay).

Guts and Ruts by Floyd S. Fierman [is a] book about Jewish-American pioneers of the Southwest, with a full chapter on Zadoc and Abraham Staab. It goes quite a lot into their business dealings and paints a portrait of Staab as a somewhat ruthless businessman. Fierman's book also has a page on Julia Staab, and it is he who reports her hair turned white suddenly after the death of her last child. He also reports she pretty much stayed in her room with a "companion" for the five years before her death. I have no reason to doubt these accounts. However, I do doubt a few of Fierman's other facts. He discounts the Cathedral story as untrue, despite the fact that there are several independent sources that vouch for the validity of it. He also says that Julia was pregnant fifteen times and lost eight children in infancy. This goes against all the family accounts I've heard of, although it's possible he's referring to miscarriages."

So, the real story of Julia Staab is, as Mr. Ach so wisely observed, more mundane and much sadder than all the sensationalized stories. She had eight children, not seven, and she battled health issues and depression. Mr. Ach's suggestion that the depression was likely postpartum is particularly observant and meaningful considering the controversies that rage even today about that enigmatic condition. Depression is a much more logical explanation for Julia's reclusive behavior than her husband confining her to her room.

The emphasis on Julia's hair turning white or premature gray – a component in every single story about Julia – is also curious and is likely to have a logical explanation as well. The color change could have been a result of Julia's health problems. Hair color happens in the follicle—or doesn't happen, as in the case of white hair. Therefore once a hair has emerged it is physically impossible for it to change color. However, a certain autoimmune disease can cause all colored hairs to fall out, leaving only white ones, but it is physically impossible for hair that was not already white or gray to turn color in a short period of time. Autoimmune disease aside, perhaps there is an even more mundane explanation. My sense is that Julia just quit "dyeing" it. Hair dye is not a modern invention; it's been around for centuries. Hair dyes of the nineteenth century were nasty brews that variously mixed phenylenediamine, henna, caustic soda, sodium carbonate, ammonia, or hydrogen peroxide. If Julia was chronically ill, perhaps it just became too much to subject herself to the smelly, toxic chemicals for the sake of vanity. Maybe what made the change of hair color so noteworthy is that a woman of Julia's social status might have been expected to dye her hair...just as women of that era were expected to wear corsets and long dresses. As the story got passed along, the shocking part—that she let her hair turn gray rather than "dyeing" it as a proper lady should—became "it turned white over a short period of time."

As for the Hebrew inscription over the door of St. Francis Cathedral, some long-time Santa Fe residents strongly dispute the story that Abraham Staab or Santa Fe's Jewish community financed its completion. One resident told me that Archbishop Lamy was simply following the tradition of other cathedrals in Europe, which included the Hebrew inscription of "Yahweh," because it was the first word of God. That seemed an intriguing theory so I searched for other instances of cathedrals with a Yahweh inscription. The only instance I could find was the Basilica of Saint Louis, the King in St.

Hebrew inscription called a Tetragrammaton on the keystone above the door of St. Francis Cathedral.

Louis, Missouri, the fourth church constructed to serve the Catholic parishioners of St. Louis completed in 1834. It too has a Hebrew inscription, Yahweh, above the main façade. Ironically, the Bishop had it inscribed as a gesture of friendship to the Jewish community.

While the factual details of Julia's life became badly distorted through the continuing embellishment and sensationalizing of her personal history, I don't believe that the truth of her life invalidates the stories of paranormal experiences at La Posada. Indeed, based on Julia's life story and details provided by Mr. Ach from his family history, I believe that there may be more than just Julia's presence lingering in the old Staab household.

Like the ghost "Earl," who inhabited my house in the North Valley of Albuquerque, some souls linger in places simply because they so loved the place and became firmly attached to the earthly energy there. Because there are sharply different accounts of events—flying glasses, disruption of remodeling efforts, trays knocked out of hands—as opposed to heat suddenly flowing through the building to warm

St. Francis Cathedral at night.

guests, my sense is that there is more than one presence in La Posada. Perhaps the accounts of benevolent "hostess" are Julia's lingering energy and the disruptive events and restless energy emanate from Julius Staab, who committed suicide. I contacted Mr. Ach again to find out if Julius may have committed suicide in the house. He said family records didn't reveal where or how Julius killed himself, only that his death was a suicide. Disruptive events during remodeling may also be Abraham manifesting his displeasure that his house was being remodeled—much like the ghost "Earl," who strongly communicated that he did not like a piece of ornate woodwork being removed.

The story of Abraham and Julia Staab is a fascinating story of New Mexico history in its own right and the evidence that they may remain in their house makes it all the more intriguing. While Abraham might not appreciate the adobe architecture that has consumed the house he had built, I believe that Julia would enjoy the lush grounds, burbling fountain, and other amenities that make the present day La Posada a world-class resort.

THE LORETTO CHAPEL

The legendary Loretto Chapel is one of Santa Fe's premier landmarks attracting tens of thousands of visitors each year, in part, because of the intriguing mystery of its "Miraculous Staircase." Despite many attempts to rationalize, explain, and discredit "The Miracle," the story endures and endears the Loretto Chapel to visitors and locals alike. But there are *other* stories...stories of paranormal encounters of a most personal and spiritual nature that have happened in the magnificent chapel.

Commissioned in 1872 by the French native who figured so prominently in Santa Fe's history, Jean Baptiste Lamy, the Loretto Chapel, with its Gothic Revival pinnacles, spires, buttresses, rose window, and dressed stone masonry, looks like it belongs in a French village, not the desert mountains of the Southwest. Indeed, it was modeled after Lamy's beloved Sainte Chapelle in Paris and would be the first Gothic structure west of the Mississippi.

By the 1870s Lamy had been elevated to Archbishop and he had ambitious plans for both the architecture of Santa Fe and the religious education of its citizens. His architectural projects included the Cathedral of St. Francis and a smaller and beautifully appointed convent chapel, to be called *Our Lady of the Light,* for the Sisters of Loretto, who ran a nearby school for girls. Building the chapel honored the Sisters of Loretto, who had endured punishing physical and emotional hardship to answer Lamy's call that they come to Santa Fe to educate the poor, Spanish-speaking children.

The order of the Sisters of Loretto was founded in Kentucky in honor of Loretto, Italy, which was, according to legend, where angels spirited the boyhood home of Jesus and the Holy Family of Nazareth to protect it during the crusades in the thirteenth century. And it was from their central Kentucky Motherhouse that the Sisters set out in the summer of 1852 first by wagon to St. Louis and then by boat up the Missouri River to Independence. Sisters Magdalen, Catherine, Hilaria, Roberta, and their Mother Superior, Matilda, then began their arduous journey west by wagon train. Mother Matilda died of cholera and was buried along the trail. The remaining sisters continued the long journey over dusty trails, enduring blazing heat in their long black wool habits and veils. They survived vexing problems such as broken axles and terrifying events such as the night Indians surrounded the wagon galloping and threatening attack before riding off and miraculously leaving the group unharmed. In September they finally arrived not at a peaceful convent like the Motherhouse they had left in verdant Kentucky, but a tiny one-room adobe hut in the wild desert frontier town of Santa Fe. Bishop Lamy appointed Sister Magdalen Mother Superior and hired Mexican carpenters to build them a convent school for girls to be called Loretto Academy, Our Lady of the Light.

Then, in 1873, Lamy hired French architect Antoine Mouly to design a chapel for the sisters. The elderly Mouly was assisted by his son, Projectus, who actually oversaw the construction. Mother Magdalen placed the project under the patronage of St. Joseph, the patron saint of carpenters, writing in the annals, "In whose honor we communicated every Wednesday that he might assist us. Of his powerful help we have been witness on several occasions."

The Loretto Chapel

Before construction was complete, Antoine Mouly died suddenly, and shortly thereafter so did Projectus. Some accounts attribute the death of Projectus to pneumonia and yet other accounts say he was shot by Bishop Lamy's nephew who accused Projectus of "philandering" with his wife.

The deaths of the architect and his son left workers in a quandary: there was no provision for access to the choir loft in the plans and, with no space available for regular stairs, the workers had no idea how the Moulys had planned to address this apparent design oversight. While it was not uncommon for churches of the time to use ladders as access to the loft— because most choirs were male—the Sisters of Loretto deemed ladder access most undignified. Mother Magdalen consulted a variety of craftsmen and none had a practical solution to their problem.

So the Sisters prayed a nine-day *novena* to St. Joseph.

On the last day of the novena an elderly stranger appeared at the chapel with a burro and a small collection of simple carpenter's tools: a hammer, a saw, and a square. He offered to build a staircase and requested only privacy and large tubs of water. When the Sisters entered the chapel for prayers, the mysterious carpenter would depart and the Sisters saw wood soaking in the large tubs although they had never seen wood delivered to the chapel. When the Sisters finished their prayers the carpenter would return. Accounts vary on the length of time it took the carpenter to complete the staircase, some say six months, others say as long as eight months. However, when the carpenter was finished, a stunning helix staircase spiraled twenty feet up to the choir loft with two complete 360-degree turns. Most remarkable was that it had no center support and was made with no nails or screws. The Sisters were delighted and planned a fine dinner to honor the carpenter, but he disappeared. Mother Magdalen checked local lumberyards to determine where he bought the wood and if anyone at those businesses might know his identity or if there was a bill for the Sisters. Nobody had seen the carpenter. No wood had been delivered and there was no bill for the Sisters. Since the carpenter left before Mother Magdalen could pay him, the Sisters offered a reward for anyone who could identify the mysterious carpenter, but no one came forward with information. Even the wood was a mystery. For years it was thought to be an exotic unknown species, but a recent analysis identifies it as being a type of spruce, most likely Engelmann, a pale, soft, flexible wood that grows only in high elevations. Still, there are some authorities that say the wood is an "edge-grained fir" or long-leaf yellow pine, neither of which is indigenous to New Mexico.

Engineers have long marveled at its impossible structural integrity. Theoretically, it should collapse into its own footprint because the entire weight of the structure was born on its base. And yet it has stood and has been used daily—there are pictures of entire choirs standing on each step, hymnals in hand. In addition, the perfect curves of the stringers are another marvel. Each has nine splices on the outside and seven on the inside. How a single man could accomplish this level of perfection, working alone with only the simplest of tools, stupefies even those with a high level of carpentry knowledge.

There have been modifications to the stairway over the years. As it was originally built, the stairway had no balustrade. Descending the staircase required considerable balance and fortitude, not only because of the two 360-degree turns, but also because of the inherent springiness of the staircase, thought to be one of the secrets of its structural integrity. A Loretto Sister, Sister Mary, delighted in telling the story that she and a young friend were among the first to climb the staircase. However, coming down was another matter. She explained that it was so disorienting to try to descend the stairs they resorted to crawling down on their hands and knees. Thirteen years after the completion of the staircase a balustrade was

The Miraculous Staircase in the Loretto Chapel.

added, itself a considerable work of craftsmanship. Also, the part of the staircase under the treads and between the stringers was not actually wood, but lime plaster strengthened with horsehair. Over the years, visitors desiring to take more than just the experience of the chapel with them had chipped away considerable chunks of the plaster. In celebration of the centennial of their arrival in Santa Fe in 1952, the Sisters had the staircase refurbished, filling in the missing pieces of plaster and painting over it to make it look remarkably like varnished wood.

The Loretto Chapel has long been a favorite subject of debunkers who detest or perhaps fear the idea that an event might not have a "logical" explanation. Still, despite many theories and analyses and claims that the carpenter was, variously, a German or French craftsman, and that wood was actually delivered, or that the staircase was actually made elsewhere and delivered to the Loretto Chapel, the chapel remains a beautiful enigma. Regardless of its origin, even the most practical-minded, miracle-adverse marvel at the astonishing level of craftsmanship and remarkable construction of the staircase.

And it was in this beautiful enigma that Richard Lindsley worked for seventeen years as chapel curator and gift shop manager. When I visited with him at San Miguel he said, "If you're interested and have some time, I can tell you something really amazing that happened to me when I worked as the curator of the Loretto Chapel. It's a rather long, but worthwhile story."

Richard explained that it was his job to open the chapel and shop each morning, turn on the lights and turn off the alarm system. At night he was the last person to leave, turning off the lights, arming the alarm, and locking the doors. He did this four days a week; another employee was responsible for opening and closing the other three days of the week.

"*It* started in 2002," Richard says, gazing off into the distance. "When I entered in the morning, there were crosses

A display of crosses in the gift shop of the Loretto Chapel.

removed from the gift shop display and scattered on the floor. We had them arranged much as they are on that wall there," he said, gesturing to an array of crosses displayed on the wall of the San Miguel gift shop. "Only it was a much, much larger display," he continued. "Every morning there would be five or six crosses scattered on the floor. These were wood crosses, ceramic crosses, plaster crosses... None were ever broken. Like clockwork...every morning for two years. At first I thought it was a joke.

"I asked the other manager if he had the same experience and he said he did." At this point Richard pauses to describe the other manager. "He calls himself 'a modern rationalist,'" Richard said with a hint of disdain. "When I suggested that it seemed more than just a little strange, he said that it was just the wind blowing them off the wall at night. But there were no open windows. Or, that something bumped the wall outside. [The walls of the chapel gift shop are two feet thick adobe.] He refused to believe the cause of the crosses on the floor was anything other than a logical event.

"Well, thank heavens I'm slow," Richard points at my notebook, "and you can write that down. 'I—WAS—**SLOW**.'" He says it again word-by-word, with emphasis on slow.

Confused, I scribble that in my notes.

"Finally, I determined that this was a spirit that wanted help," Mr. Lindsley continued. "I saw this show on TV about a woman who talks to spirits and something clicked.

"It was about a woman who ran an antique shop. Anyway, the show triggered something in me. I, as a Roman Catholic, came to the conclusion that it was a soul in Purgatory."

Richard then went on to pose an intriguing theory that Purgatory is a dimension associated with this plane—"a place where the fabric of reality is torn" and that "souls can get stuck there and not be able to move on to Paradise."

"I asked other people about the possibility of a soul trapped in Purgatory trying to communicate with me and they all dismissed the events as perhaps being 'just Sister George'."

I recognized the name Sister George as the subject of a number of stories of restless spirits. Richard tells me that Sister George was a nun who taught mentally handicapped children. "She was so dedicated to teaching them that at one point she was teaching them in a chicken coop because that was the only place available. She was also a teacher at Loretto. When strange things happen, sometimes people would jokingly say, 'It must be Sister George.' I think maybe because they liked to make fun of her name. You know how it is when people just don't want to believe."

He said that last phrase again very slowly: "*Just don't want to believe.*" I nod and wait for him to continue.

"Once I realized that it was a spirit seeking help, the next morning when I went in, before I turned on the lights, I called out, 'If there is a soul here that would like to have a Mass said, leave one cross tomorrow.' I turned on the lights and went into the gift shop. There were six crosses on the floor. I replaced them on the display and went into the chapel. When I came back into the shop, there was one cross on the floor."

I gasp as I feel every tiny hair on my body tingle. Richard and I stare at each other and he knows that I believe him and that I appreciate the profound implications of this communication with a spirit.

"At lunch I went to the Cathedral and requested a mass be said 'for the soul at Loretto Chapel.' A mass was said and the priest gave me a mass card. The next morning I went into the gift shop and there were no crosses on the floor. I said, 'I kept my promise. I had a mass said for you.' And I left the Mass card on the spot where I had found the single cross the previous morning."

Neither of us spoke. I was speechless from the power of his story.

Very softly Richard said, "It is my belief that the soul was released to Paradise." Then he laughed and said, "And I'm glad I was slow. Because it went on for two years and then abruptly stopped—I knew it was real."

I visited the Loretto Chapel to find out if anyone else who worked there had any unusual experiences. It is a profoundly peaceful and beautiful place, even with streams of tourists coming in and out. The Chapel was sold in the early seventies by the Sisters to a private enterprise that operates it as an historical attraction, charging a small admission fee. In addition, it is rented out for occasions befitting a chapel such as weddings. A recorded narration of the story of the Miraculous Staircase with lovely choir music by the Santa Fe Desert Chorale plays in a loop as people wander around looking at the staircase and marveling at the intricate stained glass windows that flood the small chapel with ethereal light. For a very brief moment, literally, I am alone in the chapel and I soak up its tranquil splendor before more tourists enter, digital cameras flashing.

I ask a young man at the gift shop if anyone has had any unusual experiences. He explains, "Oh yes, ask Vanessa. She's at the admission station." Then he adds, "They seem to happen mostly to women. I think it's because of the Sisters and all. Maybe they relate better to women."

Vanessa Schultz is eager to tell me her stories as she takes admission and tends to her duties monitoring visitors to the Chapel. She explains that she has worked at the Chapel for six years and seems almost at a loss as where to begin because, "There are just so many amazing things."

First, she explains that everyone seems to attribute the mysterious happenings to Sister George. Vanessa tells me that Sister George, during life, was known for her love and devotion to children, playing pranks, and smoking cigars.

"Cigars?" I ask.

"Oh yeah, she smoked them all the time."

Vanessa then recalls how one night she and a co-worker were cleaning and closing up after a wedding. "We had just closed the big metal gate and were leaving and we heard the gate being shaken really hard...and yelling. We looked at each other. We knew for certain we hadn't locked anyone in. It scared us and we left. Our supervisor said it was just the wind. But we knew it wasn't. The way the gate shuts, real tight with this kind of suction, there's no way the wind could shake it like that."

As with Richard Lindsley, sometimes strange things happened in the adjoining gift shop. Vanessa described a kiosk type of machine that, when certain buttons were pressed played preview selections of music that could be purchased on CD or cassette. All of the music on the kiosk were children's tunes. The machine also had a button to control the volume of the music. She said that there was one particular song that would come on when nobody was around to press the button. Not only would it begin playing by itself, the volume would increase. "It drove us nuts," she says, rolling her eyes. "We would try to turn it down and it would come back up. Always the same song. It was a song that had little children laughing and giggling in it. I don't remember what the name of it was, just that it had these little kids laughing in it. Finally we decided to just unplug the machine because there must be something wrong with it. So, we unplugged it and...*it* continued to happen! Same song. And there was no electricity!"

There was another strange incident related to music. Vanessa tells how she and a co-worker were preparing the Chapel for a late evening wedding. "We walked into the lobby here and all of a sudden the organ—there's this wooooonnnkk," Vanessa says, imitating an organ chord. "I called out 'Mark!' He's the guy that plays the organ, thinking he was trying to scare us. And then Mark and the wedding photographer come walking into the lobby from the gift shop. I told them what happened and the wedding photographer was telling me 'that's ridiculous, that's impossible' when I was telling him weird stuff happens here. He wouldn't believe us."

"So, we all went into the Chapel to continue setting up. We're all standing there and all of a sudden the organ goes off again. The photographer looked at us trying to figure out how we had done it and we tried to explain to him that we hadn't done anything. Mark was standing right there with his hands at his side. Even Mark told him weird stuff happens here, but the photographer didn't want to believe us."

At a winter wedding, Vanessa and a co-worker came in from the cold to sit in the very back of the chapel. She happened to glance up and see a light fixture spinning. She said there was no breeze in the chapel and even if there were, "It would take a huge wind to move something that big. It just kept whirling and we couldn't figure out how or why."

Vanessa speaks softly when she talks about the experiences she describes as "true blessings." She said that sometimes when she sits by herself in the Chapel she is suddenly enveloped in a small cloud of intoxicating fragrance. She says others have experienced the smell as well and describe it as a rose scent, but Vanessa insists it's hyacinths. "I can step outside the area where I was surrounded and don't smell anything. Then I can step back in and be surrounded again. It is the most beautiful, amazing smell." She goes on to describe other private moments. "Sometimes when I'm sitting there by myself, all of a sudden I'll hear beautiful singing, choir singing. It sounds like it is very, very far away, but it's right there, right in the Chapel."

"Just a couple of months ago, I had something happen that's never happened before. I was sitting in the Chapel and, out of the corner of my eye, this big gray form just sort of whooshed by me. All the other times that I've had experiences, I've never seen anything. That was the first time I ever actually saw something."

One of Vanessa's greatest joys in her job is seeing the profound emotional impact the Chapel has on other people. "It's not just us, the people who work here, who have experiences. Many people, when they come out, feel like something has wrapped them in its arms and hugged them tight, surrounding them with love. You can feel the love in there. Some people come out crying from the emotion of it. Some people come back every year on the anniversary of something special, something beautiful that happened to them when they were in the Chapel. I like seeing them and sharing that with them."

Finally, Vanessa says, "I always thank them, you know, thank you for choosing me. I talk to them. This is *their* place. *They* are not scary...*they* are kind and special. I never feel afraid."

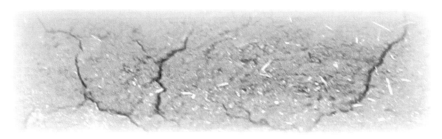

PALACE
OF THE GOVERNORS

Palace of the Governors.

Originally built in 1610, as Spain's seat of government for all lands west of the Mississippi, Santa Fe's Palace of the Governors is the oldest public building in the United States. It became the first territorial capitol when New Mexico was annexed by the United States in 1846 and was designated a registered National Historic Landmark in 1960 and an American Treasure in 1999. Since 1909 it has housed the Museum of New Mexico, an extensive collection spanning the history of Santa Fe and the Southwest.

Since the 1930s the long portal in front of the Palace has been used by Native American vendors to display their jewelry and other works of art on colorful blankets. Carefully regulated to insure quality and authenticity, the vendor program recognizes 850 authorized participants from all Native American communities and cultures in New Mexico.

The Palace was originally constructed as a true multi-purpose building. With its four-feet thick adobe walls, it served as a fortress, living quarters for Spanish officials, military barracks and stable, a chapel, and a prison. It was seized during the Pueblo Revolt and was one of the few buildings not destroyed. The pueblo people reclaimed it as their home, grinding corn on the stone floors and, in a turnabout of San Miguel being built on one of their kivas, converted the chapel to a kiva.

Ghost legends have it that at night there are sounds of moaning, praying, and other audible paranormal events. When I visited the Palace of the Governors in search of ghosts, the cordial greeter and museum ticket taker tells me that one of the night security guards had some very strange experiences. While they asked around to see when this particular security guard works, I struck up a conversation with another security guard who had overheard my request. "I bet you've heard some cool stories," he says. I reply that I have and that I have also learned some bizarre little-known stories about Santa Fe.

"Oh, yeah? Like what? My family has been here for generations. I bet I've heard whatever story you've got."

For no particular reason I decide to tell him about Abraham Staab's donation of money to finish St. Francis Cathedral and Archbishop Lamy's acknowledgement by having the Hebrew inscription Yahweh on the keystone. The young man's jaw drops. Slowly he rolls up his sleeve. On his massive bicep is a remarkable, almost photo-realistic tattoo of St. Francis Cathedral with praying hands.

"Where?" he asks, pointing to his arm. "Where is the inscription?"

"Uh well, it's right under the finger tips of the praying hands," I reply.

I finally ended up leaving my card and a note for the security guard who had the ghostly encounters, but as always seems to happen when I can't meet someone face-to-face, I never heard from him. Still, seeing the remarkable tattoo of St. Francis Cathedral was a slice of pure Santa Fe that was almost as good as a ghost story.

9

HOTEL ST. FRANCIS

I was alerted to some strange happenings at the St. Francis by a woman who once worked there, I'll call "Cary." Cary told me that late one night she, the bartender, and a customer were at the bar watching TV. She said she felt somebody pass behind her. Cary turned, expecting to see a customer sitting down at a table. There was nobody. She got up and looked around the bar area. Nobody. She said to the bartender, "Who just passed behind me? I felt somebody pass behind me. Did you see where they went?" The bartender laughed and said, "That's just the ghost lady. She always screws with me when I try to close." Cary also told me that when she was working room service there was a particular hall that she hated to go down. It gave her a very uncomfortable feeling and she didn't understand why. When she mentioned to a fellow employee that the hall gave her the creeps, she learned that a woman had committed suicide in a room in that hallway. Cary said, "The woman was very considerate. She left a note for the housekeeper warning her not to come into the bathroom so that an innocent person wouldn't discover something gruesome."

Based on Cary's tip, I visited Hotel St. Francis. Walking into the lobby is like stepping into the late 1800s. Besides the elegant furnishings that were reminiscent of another era, there is a feeling, an ambiance, of a more genteel time when instead of cars passing by on Don Gaspar, there were horses and carriages. The effect is so complete it almost seems strange to see people in modern dress, cell phones pressed to their heads, hurrying through the lobby with rolling suitcases clicking over the polished tile floor rather than women in long dresses closing their sun parasols and men with handlebar mustaches lugging leather valises.

I go up to the bar and ask the bartender about any strange happenings. He said that nothing has happened to him personally, but he has heard that some other employees have been so frightened they've run out the front door and never come back. Because he is setting up for an important event, he directs me to the concierge.

The most gracious and helpful concierge, Gloria, pauses from directing guests to nearby attractions and patiently answering their questions to consider my query about ghosts. She tells me that the person I need to speak to is Steve Hererra, the engineer. "I know he's had some really interesting experiences." However, Steve isn't around just then, but Gloria is interested in my research and remarks that while she hasn't had any experiences at Hotel St. Francis, she has had experiences at another property and her house has a resident ghost. I flip open my notebook and Gloria tells me a story that makes me nod and smile because it reminds me so much of "my" ghost "Earl."

Gloria begins by explaining that she lives on one of Santa Fe's oldest roads, Old Pecos Trail, in a neighborhood that has seen its share turmoil over the years including a murder and a suicide. "My daughter was the first to see him," Gloria says. "She was about five. She told me, 'there's a man in the house,' and I was alarmed because I thought it was a real man. She described him as wearing grey striped pants. Later, she even drew a picture of him. After that I caught glimpses of him and my husband saw him too." Gloria describes how sometimes she sees him in the corner of her eye, but one time she saw him, this time wearing brown pants and blue shirt, walk out her gate.

"I tried to get his attention, but he was completely oblivious to me, like I wasn't even there. And then he was gone," she said, shaking her head in amazement. "It's like *they* don't know we're here," she adds. Gloria said that a guest to their home had the experience of a "man" walking next to him down the hall. Again, the "man" seemed totally unaware of the human presence next to him.

"I don't know why, but we named him Gus." Gloria says. "Since he was there I figured he should have a name. And I told him, 'just don't scare me.' And he hasn't really. When I leave, I tell him to watch the house."

An Hispanic man with silvering hair strides by and Gloria says, "There's Steve. There's the man you need to talk to."

I introduce myself to Steve and he says, "Oh yes, I have some stories." He looks around and says, "But I don't want to talk about them here. And I can only give you a few minutes, I'm really busy."

"Oh come on," Gloria says. "I want to hear them too."

"No," says Steve, "I don't want to talk about this stuff with a lot of people around." He gestures to the comings and goings in the lobby.

I follow him as he threads his way through the lobby and down a long corridor to a delightful brick-paved courtyard with blue gates and heavy round iron filigree tables enameled a deep hunter green. The courtyard is empty. "Good," Steve proclaims, "We can talk here."

With the fountain burbling and birds singing on a beautiful spring afternoon, Steve tells me stories of bizarre happenings.

"Well, first there was something weird that happened with the furniture. A housekeeper told me this." He adds, "There was remodeling going on in a couple of rooms on the second floor. A bunch of furniture was piled up between two rooms. The next thing you know, all the furniture is down at the end of the hall. Nobody knew how it got there, but it wasn't a big deal—the first time. They moved all the furniture back and it ended up at the end of the hall again and nobody knows how it happened."

I think about Artie Garcia's story of boxes being unpacked at the Grant Avenue house.

Steve begins another story. "You know how there's that old-fashioned elevator in the lobby with the glass door?" Steve asks. "Well you have to look in and see if anyone is in it when it comes down before you open the gate. So, the elevator came down and I looked in and there was a lady in a long white dress with black boots. I stepped back and waited for her to come out. I waited and waited and nothing happened so I looked in the window again and there was nobody there.

"But the weirdest thing," Steve continues, "is one day I was painting a baseboard in a hallway. We had important things going on and I was in a big hurry so I was painting really quickly to get it done, and..." he adds, somewhat sheepishly, "not very carefully. There is this nicely dressed man walking down the hall. He says to me, 'you're doing a marvelous job keeping up this fine old hotel.' I thanked him. He put his card in the door. I heard it click and he went into the room right by where I was painting. A couple of minutes later Matilda from housekeeping comes up and she starts to go into the room. I tell her, 'no, Matilda, there's a guest in there.' And she says, 'This is an unoccupied room. There's nobody staying in there.' We have kind of a little argument and she just goes in. I wait to hear some kind of yelling from the guest and for her to hurry out, but nothing happens, so I get up and go in the room. Matilda says, 'See, there's nobody in here.' I tell her I saw a man come in here just a few minutes ago. You better knock on the bathroom door; he might be in there. So, Matilda knocks on the bathroom door a couple of times and nothing. We open the door and there is nobody there. So, *that* was very strange."

I nod in agreement and ask him about what the bartender told me about somebody running out and never coming back.

"Oh yeah, that was the night security guard. He went into the De Vargas room. There was a lady in a white dress floating in the air. She didn't have any feet. The guy was so freaked he ran out the front door and never came back. Supposedly, somebody saw something equally creepy in the laundry room and did the same thing—left and never came back. A lot of people get a creepy feeling in the laundry room," he adds.

"My office is down in the basement. Sometimes there are weird bumping sounds down there and the boiler room is kind of weird. My desk faces the wall and the door is to my back. I don't like people just walking in on me, so I put a mirror up over my desk. Sometimes when I've been working on the computer, I'll see something in the mirror. I'll turn around, but there's nothing there."

"That's all that's happened to me here," Steve concludes. "It's really nothing compared to what happened to me when I worked at La Residencia. I can tell you about that too if you're interested. Oh, and Casa Real, I know about some weird things there too."

10

CASA REAL & LA RESIDENCIA

Casa Real and La Residencia are health care facilities. According to Santa Fe lore, Casa Real was built over an old prison cemetery in 1985. From the time it opened visitors, employees, and patients have reported strange things happening and just a general creepy, oppressive feeling about the place. As far as specific paranormal activity, cold spots moving through rooms and sounds of moaning and crying have been reported in both the north and south wings of the building.

When Steve Herrera worked at Casa Real, the building had its own morgue. He said that when bodies were wheeled down the hall to or from the morgue the hallway lights would flash.

But Steve's best stories concerned La Residencia. Currently it is a nursing home, but once La Residencia was a hospital. According to the State of New Mexico Tourism website, "Many years ago, a little boy died in Room 311 from injuries suffered in an automobile accident. Unfortunately, the boy's father also died in the same car wreck. Today the muffled crying of the little boy is heard so often that administrators try to keep the room unoccupied.

"Other paranormal occurrences have also happened in the basement. These only began to occur when the state museum began to utilize the basement to store Indian artifacts. Reportedly, strange sounds are heard in the basement rooms so often that some nurses refuse to enter the area. On one occasion, two nurses reported seeing a wall in the basement oozing fresh blood."

Steve tells me that he worked at La Residencia twice; once when it was a hospital, "when I was younger, before I went into the service," and then again years later. He repeats some stories that the nurses told him the first time he worked there: the building caretaker hung himself in the boiler room and a security guard going down a little used stairwell found a decaying body, fled in terror, and never came back.

The first incident Steve experienced at La Residencia was during his second stint of employment, after it had become a nursing home. He said he was preoccupied, thinking about things he had to do. "I was fumbling with the keys to my office door in the basement—they always put us maintenance guys in the basement," he laughs. "There are boxes of artifacts stacked in the hall and near them I hear this banging sound. A loud banging sound. I look around, but don't see anybody. Then it happens again. Bang! Bang! Bang!" He pounds the table for emphasis. "I decide to walk very slowly down the hall and investigate. All of a sudden I feel this..." Steve abruptly reaches over and quickly touches the back of my neck. I jump.

"Yeah, that's what I did too," he says. "I figured I had to confront it so I said, 'OK, I know who you are and I don't want to play and I **AM** going to come back."

In another incident Steve says he was preparing for a fire drill for the graveyard shift, which involved sneaking into the building in the early morning hours to make sure that none of the staff saw him and would know the event was a drill. He said that he crept down to his office, turning off the lights in the hall behind him. "I turned on the light in my office and sat down at my desk to get everything ready. Then I hear the sound of boots walking in the hall, heavy steps and keys jangling. I turned and saw a light under the door. The footsteps went on down the hall. I got up and opened the door really fast, but nobody was there."

Steve explains that when the facility was a hospital, if the morgue was full, bodies were sometimes kept in the basement hallway on gurneys. "One night I'm in my office and I hear the sound of a gurney with a body on it. When you're around these places long enough, you know *that* sound. I also heard the sound of feet with those... you know those bootie things that medical people wear over their shoes. Shuffle. Shuffle. I looked and could see a shadow move by under the door. I got up and looked out when I heard it start to turn the corner. Nobody."

Steve relates another incident involving a resident. "There was this nice old guy named Jim. I really liked him. I'm up on a ladder fixing these bi-fold doors on a storage closet in the dining room and Jim pulls on my pant leg and tells me there's a sink that needs attention in the bathroom. I tell him I'll get to it when I'm finished with the door. He just stands there and then pulls on my pant leg again. I remember looking down and he had the most amazing blue eyes. He said, 'there is **REALLY** something wrong with the sink in the bathroom and you **REALLY** need to look at it **NOW**. Well, he was such a nice guy I decided I'd see what he wanted so we go to this little bathroom and I ask him, 'what's wrong with the sink?' He tells me the faucets turn on by themselves. I laughed and told him, 'no way Jim, faucets don't turn on by themselves,' and I turn to leave, but he grabs a hold of me and says, 'They do, they do. You just have to wait and see.' I don't really want to make fun of him because he was such a nice old guy, so I decide to humor him. We stand there and watch. I tell him, I don't see any water turning on. He says, 'just wait.' Finally, I sit down on the toilet and say, 'I still don't see any faucets turning on, but he tells me we have to wait, that it *will* happen. So I sit there and kind of joke with him about how long it's going to take. And we watch and watch and I'm getting restless to leave and I tell him again that faucets don't turn on by themselves and he begs me to watch just a little longer. All of a sudden the damn things **DO** turn on! I told him, 'You don't need a plumber...you need an exorcist!'"

These incidents are strange enough, but Steve's next La Residencia story is a bizarre exploration of the unseen world and lost souls.

"I was really, really busy one day getting ready for an inspection," he begins. "Two women come to the front desk and one of them asks for me by name. The front desk calls me and I tell them to tell these ladies to make an appointment and come back later because I'm really busy. The front desk calls me two more times and tells me that [the one] woman is really, really insistent that it is urgent that she talk to me and will I please come upstairs and get rid of them. I have no idea what this about and the front desk people tell me that this lady won't tell them anything besides that it is very urgent that she speak to me."

"So, I drop what I'm doing and go upstairs and I see these two women, a tall one and a shorter one. I introduce myself and the shorter one says to me 'I had a premonition...' I said, alright, we're done here and started to walk off. But she won't leave me alone. She chases after me saying, 'I had to come speak to you.' She's real persistent. I'm walking off and she's saying something about wanting to know about cold spots. And she is following me. I see I am not going to shake her, so I agree to give her five minutes. Five minutes," Steve says again for emphasis.

"We go down to the basement," he continues, "and get off the elevator. This lady starts running her hands along the wall." Steve demonstrates, miming running his palms along an invisible wall. "So we go down the hall and she's running her hands on the walls and shushing me when I ask her what she's doing. All of a sudden she jumps back and says, 'did you see that?' I think, wow, this lady is wacko. See what? I ask her and she says, 'an orb.' I don't know what the heck an orb is and I didn't see anything and I remind her she's got five minutes. We come to a closed door and she asks me, 'What's in here?' and I tell her it's a woodworking shop. We go further down the hall and she asks what's in another room and I tell her that I call it the wheelchair graveyard. She wants to go in and I tell her the light doesn't work in there."

Steve pauses and explains, "It's this room where I would stick all the broken wheelchairs. Something was wrong with the light in this room. I could never get it to work. I'd change the bulb, checked all the connections and the switch, but the bulb would just go out. I never had time to really mess with it."

"So, anyway, this lady says she wants to go in there. So I open the door and she steps in and she gasps and says, 'Oh my God! Do you see them?' See what? I ask her. 'There's a bunch of them,' she says. I don't see anything, but she tells me that this room must be where the souls cross to the other side. Her friend didn't see anything either," he adds.

Steve explains that by then he was getting rather disturbed and didn't know what to do with the woman. "Then she says to me, 'You think you're just the plant manager, but your role is much greater. You have powers. You have to help them.' Now, I am completely baffled and a little freaked out. I ask her what I am supposed to do. She tells me that I can talk to them, pray for them, or bring a priest down there. Well, I'm getting freaked out, but I'm kind of, well, you know, interested. Because it's just so weird," he adds.

"She finds another door and asks what's in there and I tell her medical archives and she moves on.

"We go on down the hall, and she asks, 'What's...' but then she grabs her chest and gasps and turns all white and starts backing up and I think she's having a heart attack or something. I ask her, 'What's wrong? What's wrong?' and finally she manages to kind of choke out, 'I have to get out of here. There's something here and it isn't human and it doesn't like women. It knows who I am and why I'm here.'"

Steve pauses and at this point Gloria, Hotel St. Francis' concierge, joins us. "I want to hear. I want to hear," she says as she sits down, "but I've only got a couple of minutes."

"I am not starting over," Steve says with a laugh.

"That's OK," Gloria says eagerly, "Go on."

"So this lady is acting like she's having a heart attack and her friend seems concerned too and I walk closer to her and she says, 'You're standing in it!' real alarmed. 'Standing it what? I ask and I'm looking around. Her friend walks closer and she says, 'Now you're standing in it.' I don't feel anything, I don't see anything, and I don't know what she's talking about, and her friend and I just kind of look at each other. But I am kind of scared for her because she does look like she's having a heart attack so we leave the area and she gets better. We go upstairs to a dayroom area. There are a lot of folks in there playing games and stuff. This woman looks in there and gasps again, and says, 'Do you see *them*?' Well, of course I don't see *them*. See what? I ask her. 'There are angels in there,' she says.

"So, by then," Steve continues, "I realize I have kind of gotten sucked into her thing and it is all very weird. I tell her, look, I gave you a lot longer than five minutes. If you want to really prove to me what you can do, and that you have some kind of *abilities*—Steve makes air quotes—I have something for you. So I take her to this hall where there used to be a door to the morgue. We stand at the end of the hall and I tell her, there used to be a morgue here. Find it. So she goes along the wall with her hands and finally she stops. 'There's your morgue,' she says. And she was exactly right."

She left and I never saw her again and I have no idea who she was.

"Darn, I have to go," Gloria says, standing up to leave and shaking her head in disbelief.

Steve tells me that night when he went home, he told his wife what happened and asked her if they had any holy water.

"The next morning, I took the holy water and went in extra early. I went to the rooms and made the sign of the cross and prayed there — Hail Marys, Our Fathers — just prayed and blessed it. I also took my Polaroid camera and took pictures. Of the twenty-four, only two came out. I took one picture down the hall and you could see eyes in it staring back at you. The other one I took was where the lady was freaking out. When you look at it with a magnifying glass there is like this little orb and a glowing spider web."

Steve pauses and settles back in his chair.

"You know after that, I don't know how to explain it, I just felt better there. A while later I told my assistant, Juan, to change the light bulb in the wheelchair graveyard, to see if we could get it to work. He came back and said the bulb didn't need to be changed because the light was fine. I couldn't believe it. I went in there and I turned it on and off about twenty times. I just couldn't believe it. I thought, 'this is crazy!'"

11

EL DELIRIO
& THE SCHOOL
OF AMERICAN RESEARCH

The former home of sisters Elizabeth and Martha White is now the Administration building of the School of Advanced Research.

They were unconventional wealthy heiress sisters who accomplished great acts of philanthropy. Yet, somehow, a rumor characterized them as devil-worshippers who buried human sacrifice victims on the magnificent estate they carved out of a dry, rugged Santa Fe hillside and built on top of an ancient Indian pueblo.

Perhaps it was the name of their estate, El Delirio (the madness), that conjured up visions of questionable activities. Or, maybe it was the fact that the sisters, from their early years as activists in the women's suffrage movement, developed very independent lives in a time when women were expected to marry and raise a family. They were champions of a cause many of their time deemed radical: Indian rights. Whatever the misconceptions about the White sisters, Elizabeth and Martha, in reality they were remarkable women who led fascinating lives and, with their shrewd and forward-looking real estate strategies, were key players in making Santa Fe what it is today. It seems they are still very present even now, watching over their beloved estate, which, upon Elizabeth's death was donated to the School of American Research.

Amelia Elizabeth (who was always called Elizabeth), Martha Root, and Abby McDougall White were born into wealth and privilege in New York, daughters of influential newspaper magnate and businessman, Horace White. Their mother, Amelia Jane McDougall, died in 1883 when Elizabeth was only five years old. An Irish nanny raised the girls, but their father played a very active role in their lives, encouraging a good education, travel, and adventure as the girls got older. When she was sixteen, Elizabeth traveled to Paris to study French as well as Egyptian history and made detailed sketchbooks of her travels. She enrolled in Bryn Mawr, studied the classics as well as Greek, Spanish, French, and German. She graduated in 1901. Elizabeth and Martha traveled in Europe and Central America, became fascinated with other cultures, and adopted the same passionate causes of human and animal rights their father championed.

Elizabeth served as a Red Cross volunteer nurse in France in 1916. In letters, her father expressed extreme pride in her service, praising her for "working to relieve human suffering in a distant land." Three months after that letter her father died and Elizabeth returned to New York for the funeral. She went back to France and Belgium several months later, this time with her sister Martha, and Abby remained in New York to tend the vast White estate and finances. In addition to her nursing duties, Elizabeth also worked to raise money for hospitals and the Queen of Belgium decorated Elizabeth for her leadership and service.

Returning home in 1918, Elizabeth and Martha applied their passion and fundraising tactics to Indian affairs when they learned of the 1921 introduction of legislation by New Mexico Senator Holm Bursum that would allow settlers to acquire Pueblo land with no compensation to the tribes. Appalled by the injustice of what was known as the Bursum Bill, the White sisters established one organization and were instrumental in several others that opposed the legislation. They rallied prominent writers and artists to their cause. Martha took over the Metropolitan Opera House for a benefit performance of Othello and Elizabeth saw to correspondence with lawyers fighting to protect Pueblo land. The Bursum Bill was ultimately defeated, but during the process of working with Pueblo and other Native people Elizabeth recognized that their greatest needs were adequate health care and income from means that would allow them to maintain their cultural integrity.

Elizabeth White became a champion of Indian arts, establishing methods for the sale of art and crafts at a fair price that also preserved authenticity. After becoming so involved in these causes, the sisters decided to move to Santa Fe. They purchased a plot of land on Garcia Street and lived in a tiny, primitive two-room house while they oversaw construction of their grand estate. Meanwhile, they also began investing in Santa Fe real estate, forming De Vargas Development Corporation with a goal of insuring that their adopted city would forever maintain its unique architectural style and charm.

The White sisters named their estate "El Delirio" after a favorite place in Spain. It seemed that when the sisters were traveling in Seville they always managed to get lost, but would eventually find their way to a strange bar, El Delirio. "Whenever we found El Dilirio," Elizabeth would later explain, "we knew we were home."

Architect William Penhallow Henderson designed El Delirio, incorporating many aspects of both Native American and Hispanic architecture spiced with accents of Moroccan and Spanish influence. The main home of the sisters was styled after the mission at Laguna Pueblo. It became the gathering spot for all manner of artists, writers, anthropologists, and archeologists as well as the social center for all the sisters' favorite causes. In its forty by twenty-five foot living room, called The Chapel, they held festive fundraising events, grand parties, and elaborate costume balls. They even wrote and

A current view of the interior of "The Chapel." It now serves as the boardroom for the School of Advanced Research.

performed plays and held concerts at The Chapel. An eccentric butler named Knut, who had a passion for keeping things just so, managed El Delirio.

Besides their philanthropic activities, the sisters established the Rathmullen Kennels at El Delirio, named after a castle they had visited in Ireland. They hired a noted dog trainer to show the prize Irish wolfhounds and Afghan hounds they raised.

The early 1930s were the glory days of El Delirio and the White sisters. Elizabeth, by then known to all as "Miss E," helped her friend Mary Cabot Wheelwright establish what would become the famous Wheelwright Museum. Both sisters worked on their favorite causes of Native American arts and philanthropy. Elizabeth believed that Native American art had "a vitality not found in European art" and delighted that each piece seemed infused with spirit. She worked diligently for recognition of the art and to advance the artists that made it. She had a vast personal collection from all over America from Plains beadwork, to San Ildefonso pottery, to Navajo jewelry. Elizabeth's favorite quotation about Indian art is a mirror of her deep attachment to it and her worldview in general.

"I once inquired of a woman of Nambé [Pueblo, north of Santa Fe] how she would begin making an embroidered mantle. 'First of all,' she said, 'I would feed cornmeal of all colors to the butterflies, because they know how to make themselves beautiful.'"

During the height of the good times at El Delirio, Martha learned she had cancer. Perhaps because of Martha's illness, the celebrations increased since that was the character of the spirited sisters. Because Martha had become a Christian Scientist, she refused all methods of conventional medicine. She died in 1937 at age fifty-seven.

Elizabeth was heartbroken. Her sister had been the witty, fun-loving, earthy one; the one, when thrown from a horse, jumped back on laughing. Martha's outgoing nature balanced Elizabeth's more cerebral style and the two made a great team. Martha was cremated and her ashes placed in a niche in El Delirio's large gazebo

Elizabeth went on a philanthropy binge divesting herself of most of her vast personal collection of Native American art. She gave the city of Santa Fe an animal shelter in honor of Martha. When famous sculptor Francois Toretti was commissioned to do a relief sculpture of muse for the New York City Library, he modeled the central muse after Martha's face and sent a cast of it to Elizabeth, who had it recast in stone and placed on El Delirio's gazebo.

Elizabeth withdrew from public life for several years, moving into Martha's bedroom, the smallest room in the house. It contained a tiny red chair that the girls, in their childhood, had pretended was a prairie fire.

Eventually, Elizabeth emerged from her mourning, her strong sense of purpose renewed, and she again became involved in philanthropic activities. During World War II, Elizabeth served briefly as the regional director of Dogs for Defense and converted the Rathmullen Kennels at El Delirio into a training facility for service dogs for the war effort.

The long and remarkable life of Elizabeth White came to an end on August 28, 1972, her 94th birthday. Her pallbearers were the devoted gardeners of El Delirio who followed Elizabeth's guidance in transforming the desert into beautiful terraced gardens.

The School of American Research, the institution that converted El Delirio into a lovingly preserved, magnificent educational facility and retreat, changed its name to the School of Advanced Research in 2007 in honor of its centennial. From the bizarre stories I read about the School of Advanced Research, I expected it to be a rather run-down spooky place with the hostile presence of the White sisters. I read two accounts of a visiting Hopi weaver experiencing inexplicable dread of malevolent presence in the billiard room. There was a story about a student's suicide in one of the buildings, footsteps when nobody was present, hushed and murmuring voices. There were reports of one professor always feeling someone was reading over her shoulder, her office door open in the morning when it was closed the night before, and the strange behavior of her dog growling at unseen things when she brought him at night.

The School of Advanced Research was exactly the opposite of what I expected based on these stories. It is one of Santa Fe's hidden gems with amazing grounds that are a tribute to what the White sisters must have always envisioned they would be one day: towering trees shading a sprawling campus of beautiful architecture; apricot trees of proportions so large they seemed surreal; and everywhere carefully laid stone work terraces. An ambiance so peaceful and welcoming I could easily imagine just sitting under one of the venerable trees all day soaking in the tranquility.

Entering the Reception Building, a man working on a computer at the front desk asked if he could provide assistance. I told him my quest: supernatural or ghostly experiences. He laughed and said, "Well, I do know that nearly every Halloween kids from the high school jump the fence in the back and scare themselves. But as far as ghosts, you need to ask Laura, she's the librarian." He offers to walk me over to the library and, as I walk with him, he remarks, "I did hear a legend that if you stick your fingers in the eye of the statue, you will hear a scream from somewhere on the campus. I don't know if some of the visiting scholars started that story or where it came from. I never tried it," he added.

I remark that it sounded like a typical campus legend, a lot like the legend of the stone statue of a woman holding a dove on the campus of New Mexico Tech in Socorro. "The legend goes," I tell him, "that if a virgin ever graduates from New Mexico Tech, the dove will fly away."

The library is very traditional New Mexico architecture with large log viga ceilings and deep-set windows. Laura is very pleasant and smiles when I ask about ghosts. "I like to think of

Santa Fe as fifty square miles surrounded by reality," she says with a laugh. While she had no experiences at the School of Advanced Research, she said she did have experiences when she worked at the Laboratory of Anthropology on Museum Hill. She hated working late because "there was just this feeling. It was so creepy. I had a colleague. We didn't get along at all. But if we both had to work nights, we stuck together." Laura looks thoughtful and says, "I did hear that sometimes the visiting scholars will get very uncomfortable in their room and ask to be moved. Oh, and there is a woman in the administration building who says she has developed a personal relationship with a ghost she thinks is Elizabeth White."

I thank Laura for her time and wander around the sprawling campus. I find a stone staircase that leads up to a terrace where the famed dog cemetery is located. I had read that the cemetery contained "more than a dozen" dog graves. As I mount the last step, I am startled by the size of the cemetery. I count *forty-seven* graves, each marked with a two-by-four painted a pale blue. The animal's name is carved in the wood and painted orange. Each two-by-four is attached to a metal fence post making the marker look somewhat like a cross.

The dog cemetery *did* have a rather ominous look. I was also baffled by the names on the markers. There were common names like "Jamie" and "Sandy." However, most of the names were foreign sounding and not the types of names that I can imagine calling out to a dog, like "here, Amanullah!" or "fetch, Imederrine!" Some of the names were baffling, like "kitten." Was it a kitten or did one of the prize hounds have an identity crisis? When I saw a grave marked "Peter," I remembered one story I had read that said, "It is rumored that more than pets are buried there."

I sat down at the picnic table at the edge of the dog cemetery and listened to the birds. I looked over at the gazebo with the bust of Martha facing the cemetery and the grave that held the body of Elizabeth and the ashes of Martha. I looked around at all the trees and the immaculately tended gardens.

Steps to the Dog Cemetery.

Some of the forty-seven animal graves at the dog cemetery of El Delirio.

I could feel it.

This place was so loved by the sisters and they are still loving it. I could feel their presence. They enjoy people enjoying the beauty. I'm startled to realize that where I'm sitting must be the spot I read about in one of the accounts of ghosts—the only positive account: "...one teacher felt watched sitting near the gazebo but her feelings were that the spirit was content with its legacy." Yes, contentment—it described perfectly the feeling I sensed from the presence.

I walk over to the bust of Martha on the gazebo. The old gal—as a bust—has seen better days. It's almost as if the stone aged like a person, but instead of wrinkles it has cracks, which give it a very imposing presence, particularly the deep-set eye sockets. I wonder if they are deep-set from having curious fingers poked into them on Halloween. One eye in particular seems a little strange, a little more damaged.

I walk down a long stone walkway between a dense hedge of lilacs and imagine what an amazing experience it must be to

Bust of Martha Root White cast from the original central muse at the New York City Library by Francois Toretti.

stroll down that walkway on a spring evening when the lilacs are in full bloom.

I come to the formidable and very church-like original home of the White sisters, the center for all their magnificent parties and now the administration building for the School of Advanced Research. I pause outside and marvel at gigantic trumpet vines, the main stems the size of tree trunks, growing up the long windowed portal in the courtyard and spreading to both ends. They must have been just little sprouts when the sisters were living there.

Inside the Administration building I wander down the halls looking for the woman who Laura told me had a personal relationship with "Elizabeth's" ghost, a woman I'll call "Anna." When I find her, she invites me into her cozy office and gestures for me to sit in a specific chair of a pair of equipale chairs. An equipale chair is a very traditional Mexican chair with a half-barrel shape and split cedar slats supporting a seat and backrest of tanned, stretched pigskin. These particular equipales also have accents of delicate sticks connecting the back to the seat. As I settle into the chair and open my notebook, the chair makes the characteristic squeaky sounds that are supposed to be part of the charm of equipales.

Anna tells me that her office used to be Elizabeth's room after Martha's death. "She makes her presence known with the chair," Anna says, pointing to the other equipale chair next to me. "I'll be sitting at my desk and all of a sudden it squeaks just like somebody sat down in it. Just like when you sat down. Then, periodically, it squeaks like somebody is shifting around it in. It usually happens in the afternoon."

It is very difficult to sit quietly in an equipale chair because they squeak with the tiniest movement. But certainly, they could never squeak from say a gush of air in the room or the movement of people.

"At first it was strange," Anna continues, "but then it started happening more frequently. So, when I'd hear it, I'd say, 'hello Elizabeth.'"

I stare expectantly at the chair, hoping it will squeak, but it remains silent.

"Now she visits a couple of times a week. And one time," Anna turns to demonstrate, "I was working on the computer like this. I was actually writing something about the White sisters. Suddenly, the chair started squeaking—squeaky, squeaky, squeaky—very insistently. I looked at what I had written, reworked something, and the chair stopped squeaking. It was like she was looking over my shoulder, and disagreed with what I had written and let me know by squeaking the chair."

I ask Anna about some of the other stories I've heard; how doors that were locked would be unlocked, and how it seemed like a ghost liked to tidy up or clean. She hasn't heard about the cleaning up part, but Anna remarks that things do seem to get inexplicably rearranged, "but nothing is ever taken, just moved around."

I've read that some people have gotten very uncomfortable feelings and ask if she's had any unpleasant experiences. Anna says no, that it's a very peaceful place. Everything Anna tells me, and everything I feel, seems completely contradictory to the more darker stories of the School of Advanced Research.

Anna says, "Would you like to see the main living room? We use it as a board room now." She unlocks the door and turns on the lights in a huge room with a beautiful loft and staircase at one end. Although the former "Chapel" is now dominated by a long boardroom-type table it's easy to imagine what a great space it must have been for parties with musicians playing in what the sisters dubbed the choir loft. I remark to Anna that the loft also looks like a cozy place to read. She tells me that in the loft is a special large cupboard with a unique dictionary set that has special holders for each book. "You pull the book out for one letter and it falls open in this amazing holder. It's gigantic."

As Anna leads me out of The Chapel, she points out a large map that is under glass in the hallway. It is an almost cartoon-like drawing of the entire El Delirio estate. Anna points out the details: "Here's someone calling out, 'Sandy! Sandy!' Sandy was the sisters' small dog," she explains. "See, here's the parrot sitting on a stand in the courtyard echoing 'Sandy! Sandy!'" Anna explains Gustave Baumann, one of Santa Fe's premier artists, drew the pictorial map in 1927.

Anna points out her other favorite details on the map: "Look, here's the label on a statue, 'New Mexican Bookworm,' sometimes called the plumed serpent guarding the library. And look at this," She points to a tiny picture at the bottom of the map of two men looking at a pile of bricks with the caption, *Vay Morley and Joe Spinden excavating "an old pueblo site."* I note the quotation marks around the phrase old pueblo site. Anna tells me Morely and Spinden were famous archeologists. She also points to the labels, *First Prairie Dog Village, Second Prairie Dog Village,* and I recognize them as a gentle spoof on the names of the Hopi mesas—First Mesa, Second Mesa...

"And here look at this." Anna points to a drawing of a Mayan ceremony taking place in the upper part of the map. "The first swimming pool in Santa Fe was built at El Delrio. It was aboveground and they had it designed as a kind of Mayan pyramid. They had a big party when it opened and everyone dressed up like Mayans. People marched up the steps like they were being sacrificed."

Like they were being sacrificed....

So there it was. I realize that this whimsical map that depicted not only the layout of, but also the activities at, El Delirio was the source of some of the stories. How did a theme party concocted by sisters who loved pageantry get twisted into a dark tale of devil worship and human sacrifice? And the "old pueblo site." It was not that it was an actual archeological site, but rather a spoof on the way archeologists are always looking for signs of earlier habitation.

Anna offers to walk out with me and describe some of her favorite things about the School of American Research along the way. We walk down a wide flagstone path and she points

Spiral water course at El Delirio.

out the largest native locust tree I ever seen. A tree of mythic proportions compared to ones that struggle to reach ten or twelve feet in height in the wild, this locust towers several stories high with a trunk like a redwood. Anna tells me, "You should see pictures of this place when the sisters first started it. It was all desert...for years." I look around at the shady, wooded grounds in awe.

As we continue up the stone walk, I remark that the dog cemetery was a little strange and the names were odd. "Oh yes. The sisters named the Irish wolfhounds with Celtic names and the Afghan hounds with, well, Afghan names." Anna pauses and points at some stone terraces planted with blooming native plants. "These are the ceremonial corn terraces in the Gustave Baumann map." Anna scowls very slightly and says, "I don't know that the sisters would like how they are planted now, with these particular plants." I wonder if that is Anna's opinion or Elizabeth and Martha's opinion.

Anna tells me how one night there was a very expensive party at the School of Advanced Research, the kind of event where tickets are hundreds of dollars. She was working late and curious about the goings on. She points to a high terrace with lots of vegetation. "So, I was kind of sneaking around on the walk up there and I must have tripped one of the motion detector security lights because all of a sudden, I'm in the spot light."

As we reach the Reception Center, Anna mentions that it sits on the site where the Mayanesque swimming pool used to be. Snuggled up close to the building is a mammoth apricot tree towering up nearly two stories. In the high desert with unpredictable spring weather that can be eighty degrees one day and twenty the next, fruit from early blooming trees like apricots is a near miraculous event. I ask Anna if the tree ever bears fruit and she says it does more than one might think and that one reason the swimming pool was torn down is that the tree dropped so much fruit in it the pool became disgusting and nearly impossible to clean up. "Also, you don't want to sit out here or park your car anywhere near here when it has fruit because the tree is so huge and has so much fruit, it's like they shoot out of the tree. You literally get pelted with it," she says with a laugh.

Martha? I wonder.

I thank Anna for her time, the stories of her encounters with Elizabeth, and the guided tour. She recommends I buy the book in the reception center, *El Delirio: The Santa Fe World of Elizabeth White*. I have been so captivated by the presence of the sisters and their work at creating such a magnificent retreat and knowledge center, I gladly buy it.

That evening, as I peruse the book, I smile at the fascinating life the sisters must have led. There are pictures of the "human sacrifice victims" in elaborate feathered headdresses hamming it up for the camera; interior pictures of The Chapel with a cozy circular seating arrangement of over-stuffed chairs and couches instead of an imposing boardroom table; a picture of Elizabeth on the Santa Fe Plaza wearing a stylish cloche hat and holding the leashes of four wolfhounds that stand nearly to her waist and clearly outweigh her by hundreds of pounds. And, most amazing, are the many early pictures of El Delirio. It is just like Anna said: no large trees...just bare hillside and you can almost feel the harsh sun beating down in the old black and white prints. So unlike the lush grounds, the desert oasis, and scholarly retreat that the School of Advanced Research is today. I think about the old proverb: "Plant a tree under which whose shade you never expect to sit." That's exactly what the White sisters did. And while the sisters may not be sitting in the shade, they are certainly enjoying it.

12

SANTA FE
INDIAN SCHOOL

W hat if ghosts are not just the residual energy or energetic manifestation of those who have died? What if ghosts are also the residual energy of repeated and horrific trauma that occurred in the same place over decades? British paranormal author and ghost expert Peter Haining lists as one of his Five Basic Explanations for Apparitions: *"That they [apparitions] are the result of great mental conflict which has imprinted a 'photograph on the astral light' which anyone with the slightest glimmer of psychic faculty can perceive."*

And in few places has there been more "great mental conflict" than the Santa Fe Indian School, considered by some to be one of the most haunted places in Santa Fe. For decades children at the school suffered horrendous emotional and physical abuse. Disturbing energies lingering at the Santa Fe Indian School include the far away sounds of agonized screaming and shadows of hanging bodies on dimly lit walls.

But to truly understand a haunted site of this type, to recognize why many people who enter the empty rooms at the Santa Fe Indian School feel an eerie presence, it's first necessary to understand that for decades children were terrorized and abused there, perhaps, as Haining describes it, imprinting their anguish and terror on the astral light so that even those who have no "glimmer of psychic faculty" experience it.

The Santa Fe Indian School was founded as part of an official national policy in the late nineteenth century that sought to neutralize the Native population by stripping Native people of their culture, language, and spiritual traditions in order to assimilate them into the dominant culture. This new policy was championed by Colonial Richard H. Pratt who served from 1867 to 1875 in Indian Territory as an officer of the 10th Cavalry, commanding a unit of African American Buffalo Soldiers and Indian Scouts. He developed a philosophy he called "kill the Indian, save the man," which he described as the way to solve the "Indian Problem" without further bloodshed. Plus, there was the issue of Native people simply taking up too much space. As Commissioner of Indian Affairs, Thomas J. Morgan noted, "A wild Indian requires a thousand acres to roam over while an intelligent man will find a comfortable support for his family on a very small tract...Barbarism is costly, wasteful, and extravagant. Intelligence promotes thrift and increases prosperity."

So, "kill the Indian, save the man" became a philosophy widely lauded by progressive people of the day. Pratt lobbied Washington and wealthy supporters to begin an experiment that would validate his philosophy that cultural extermination would ultimately be more successful than physical extermination in dealing with Native people.

That cultural extermination began with children.

Boasting, "In Indian civilization I am a Baptist because I believe in immersing the Indians in our civilization and, when we get them under, holding them there until they are thoroughly soaked," Pratt convinced the Secretary of the Interior and the Secretary of War to give him the Carlisle barracks at a deserted military base in central Pennsylvania to start a boarding school that would "transfer the savage-born infant to the surroundings of civilization, and he will grow to possess a civilized language and habit."

The Carlisle Indian School was founded in 1879. Pratt's founding principals for Carlisle, "left in the surroundings of savagery, he [a native child] grows to possess a savage language, superstition, and life," and "Carlisle has always planted treason to the tribe and loyalty to the nation at large," greatly appealed to government officials weary of funding costly military campaigns against the Indians in the West. More boarding schools were quickly established, including the Santa Fe Indian School, which was founded in 1890. Within twenty years there were 485 schools. The Bureau of Indian Affairs (BIA) controlled twenty-five off-reservation boarding schools while churches, funded by the government, ran 460 Christian schools. Boarding school attendance was mandatory. Government officials forcibly took children from their parents or coerced parents to give up children they had hidden from Indian Agents by cutting off rations to the family. Children were shipped as far away from their homes and tribes as possible to discourage possible escapes and to make parental visits nearly impossible.

Conditions at the boarding schools were harsh and brutal. Children had their long hair sheared off. Accustomed only to soft moccasins, sandals, or going barefoot, they were forced to wear hard shoes. From never being concerned about clothing, they were forced to wear uniforms and keep them crisp with buttons polished. However, most horrifying were the beatings or having their mouths washed out with soap or even lye for speaking their native language—even when they had no knowledge of the English language. They were assigned "pronounceable" names, or in some cases, just numbers.

Another strategy for destroying the children's cultural attachments was to Christianize them, which was why the government outsourced the majority of boarding schools to churches. Children were forced to recite Bible verses and forbidden from practicing any of their spiritual traditions under threat of severe punishment.

Boarding schools received minimal funding so malnutrition and even starvation was not uncommon. Illness was rampant, partly due to lack of healthcare resources and close quarters of the dormitories and partly because the Native children had little resistance to communicable diseases such as small pox and measles. A macabre feature of all boarding schools was a cemetery. In the case of the Santa Fe Indian School, not only was there a cemetery but also reports of mass graves for small pox victims near the current location of a track.

The boarding school emphasis on cultural extermination continued unexamined until the 1920s. First, came the Indian Citizenship Act of 1924 that recognized Native people as citizens of the United States and that states could grant them voting rights. However, they would not actually receive this right for decades. (Even after the heroic efforts of Navajo Code Talkers in World War II, Native people would not be allowed to vote until 1948 in Arizona, 1953 in New Mexico, and 1956 in Utah.) Then, in 1928, a scathing report entitled "The Problem of the Indian Administration" (the Meriam Report) revealed that boarding schools were plagued with inadequate salaries, unqualified teachers, and almost non-existent healthcare and that, uniformly, boarding schools failed to improve the lives of Native people and in fact had created adults more dependent on government assistance than those who remained in their Native cultures.

Incredibly, even though cultural extermination proved to be a failure the boarding school model of education for Native children continued, only slightly modified, until the early 1970s. Native children were still taken from their families to live at boarding schools, but the actual education of children was often outsourced to local schools where children would be forced to endure daily taunting and humiliation by their classmates. I saw this taunting firsthand. The junior high and high school I attended in Albuquerque in the early 1960s had a small cadre of Native students who would arrive each day on a battered old school bus from The Bordertown Project at the Albuquerque Indian School, which had recently merged with the Santa Fe Indian School. Eyes downcast, the students would make their way through halls and classroom as the ever-present butt of jokes for their simple, unstylish clothing, their shyness, their speech patterns, and, incredibly, because they would eat every morsel of food on their lunch trays in the cafeteria. Two boys ran away in an attempt to return to their families on the Navajo reservation during Christmas break. They made it on foot almost to Gallup, some ninety miles to the west, when they were caught in a fast-moving blizzard and froze to death.

Recounting the experiences of boarding schools, decades after the fact makes grown Native men and women weep. Yet, in an article in *Amnesty Magazine*, journalist Andrea Smith recalled the history of the boarding schools: "Native scholars describe the destruction of their culture as a 'soul wound,' from which Native Americans have not healed. Embedded deep within that wound is a pattern of sexual and physical abuse that began in the early years of the boarding school system."

The emotional abuse of innocent children may be morally repugnant today, but for years it was considered standard operating procedure for Indian Boarding Schools. Today the Santa Fe Indian School has moved from its original campus and the old dormitories and classrooms are largely vacant. There is one entrance into the campus that is staffed by a security guard. I visited the campus on a Saturday afternoon and asked the security guard, a Native man who appeared to be in his mid-twenties, if had heard any stories of strange occurrences at the school. I knew that this might be a delicate topic because some Native cultures, such as the Navajo, have a strong taboo regarding the discussion of death and ghosts. The man replied that both he and his parents were alumni of the school and that they had never heard of strange occurrences. I asked specifically about the stories of far off sounds of screaming or the shadows of hanging bodies. He shook his head slowly, replying that no, he hadn't heard of such things. He also didn't know about the location of a cemetery or mass grave, but allowed that administrators probably wouldn't reveal such things to students.

We talked about the whole boarding school culture and he said that by the time his parents attended things had started to improve and he didn't feel like his experience was terrible. However, he was very familiar with the horror stories and said that he had recently learned about investigations into things that had happened many years ago at a Canadian boarding school when an electric chair and mass grave was discovered when the school was being remodeled.

I asked if I could take some pictures of the old dormitories and he said that he wasn't allowed to let anyone onto that part of the campus and I would have to get permission from the superintendent's office to take pictures. He wrote down the number for me. As several long time Santa Fe residents predicted, my calls for clarification about the history of the school, possible strange happenings, and request to take pictures were never returned.

13

Restaurant Ghosts

What is it about restaurants and ghosts in New Mexico? Perhaps it's because so many old adobe homes are converted into restaurants and the spirits stick around because of the great smells and convivial activity. Or perhaps it's because restaurants tend to have an on-going stream of visitors and staff turnover, increasing the odds of encounters between spirits and those more sensitive or receptive to their presence. Such is the case in Santa Fe where ghostly activity has occurred in a number of restaurants that were once homes in the oldest parts of Santa Fe.

Analco Barrio

Upper Crust Pizza

Directly west of the Oldest House is an old house-like building that also dates from the 1600s. It has housed many things, but currently it's the home of Upper Crust Pizza and has been since 1979. This building is supposed to be part of the "Energy Vortex." If there was ever any bad energy associated with that building, I would think that many years of incredible, delicious aromas would have negated it. Upper Crust is renown both locally and nationally for its pizza. According to the stories, two ghosts, Cowboy Jack and The Lady, inhabit the Upper Crust Pizza building.

I visited Upper Crust Pizza just as the lunch rush was winding down and asked the friendly man behind the counter if anyone had any strange experiences. He said he had heard that "a long time ago some people did," but added that he had worked at Upper Crust for ten years and had never experienced anything. "What about anybody else working here?" I asked

"Nobody in the ten years I have worked here has had any kind of strange experience and nothing weird has happened."

The Pink Adobe

The Pink Adobe began its many lives as a military barrack. A Santa Fe landmark that locals call The Pink, it has everything you would expect in a Santa Fe restaurant: legendary food; a maze of intimate little rooms; rustic furniture; creaky plank floors in one part, brick floors in another; a charming courtyard; a live

The Pink Adobe is known by locals as "The Pink."

ancient tree growing up out of one corner of the bar through the roof; and...a couple of ghosts.

The Pink Adobe and its bar, The Dragon Room, sit opposite each other with a brick courtyard in the middle. I wandered into the Dragon Room on a slow Saturday afternoon. It's peaceful and quiet—a stark contrast to its nighttime ambiance when it is raucous with laughter, blaring music, and clinking glasses and conversations shouted over the din.

I had found no references to The Pink Adobe in any of the many listings of Santa Fe ghosts, but it seemed like, being in such close proximity to San Miguel, there might be something going on. I explain to the bartender that I'm looking for ghosts and ask her about any possible strange occurrences.

"Oh yeah, there are ghosts," bartender Sabra proclaims with a laugh.

The lone patron at the bar, hunched over his Margarita, chimes in. "It's Rosalea. She used to sit right over there," he gestures to a curved banco in one corner of the bar, "with her dogs. That was her place. That's where she always sat. Some people still see her there."

"Rosalea?" I ask, scribbling.

"Yeah, she owned the Pink Adobe. She started it. She had like nine husbands," Sabra responds, adding, "She died in 2000, I think."

I ask the bar patron if he's ever seen Rosalea—the ghost. "Not the ghost, although I know people who *have* seen the ghost. Just Rosalea in real life. She was a character. She would run over our motorcycles by accident when she'd back out. Her BMW was always in the shop because she'd ding it up running over motorcycles or hitting the corner of the wall on that tight turn in and out of the parking lot in back. All this art," he turns and gestures to walls lined with paintings bursting with color and geometric shapes and stylized animals, "it's all her work."

I ask Sabra if she's had any experiences. "Not me. But plenty of people here have. As far as ghosts, I leave them alone—and

The Dragon Room bar across the courtyard from The Pink Adobe. The bar was built around the tree that grows out of the roof.

"She [Rosalea] used to sit right over there with her dogs. That was her place. That's where she always sat. Some people still see her there."

they leave me alone." She states matter-of-factly, adding, "Actually there are two ghosts. There was one long before Rosalea."

Sabra tells me that when the construction crew was digging the foundation of the Dragon Room they found a skull surrounded by potshards. Anthropologists identified it as a female from the thirteenth century. "Now, I don't know if that is the woman who is the ghost, but there is a female ghost. Her name is Mesera. Weird stuff happens over at the restaurant here, I'll show you where."

Sabra leads me across the courtyard to The Pink Adobe and we weave back through several small rooms to a cozy little room with four small tables. There are no diners in the room, but from long-ago gigs as a waitress, I instantly imagine what a tight squeeze it would be to serve in such a tiny space. Sabra points to a curio shelf painted pink with a variety of small knick-knacks. "Those things," she gestures, "move all over the place when nobody is around. This is where she seems to hang out the most...*in this corner*. They say she wears all brown."

Sabra says she has to get back to the bar, but to come back and talk to her after I finish taking pictures. She introduces me to LaDonna, who tells me, "There were a couple of real macho waiters who used to make fun of the stories of Mesera and said it was impossible, until they actually saw her and it scared the hell out of them. Now, we don't tell new employees, we just let them figure it out." Then she adds, "Mesera means waitress." LaDonna says that guests will sometimes experience Mesera. "One night we were really busy and, as these four people were leaving, they asked me, 'What is going on in that room? Our table levitated!'"

LaDonna tells me her son used to work as a dishwasher and he didn't like to work late at night because it felt weird and uncomfortable. With a sigh, LaDonna adds, "She doesn't seem as active as she used to be. Nothing has happened in awhile."

When I go back over to the Dragon Room, Sabra has another story for me about one of the other bartenders. "John saw her one night, kind of whoosh by the hallway," she says pointing into a hallway to another room in the bar. "And she whispered in his ear." She pulls a book off a shelf above the bar and hands it to me. "This has a bunch of information about Rosalie, about Mesera." She hands me *The Pink Adobe Cookbook*.

I read that the Pink Adobe was opened by colorful Cajun expatriate artist Rosalea Murphy in 1944. Writing in the preface to the *The Pink Adobe Cookbook*, Rosalea Murphy says, "By 1944 I was trying to function as an independent individual and artist. So, as an alternative to getting a time-consuming job, what better solution was there but to open a restaurant? Then I could paint, cook, and support myself under the same roof."

The cookbook describes Rosalea's love of motorcycles, horseracing, casinos, and her dogs, Don Juan and Gina Lollobrigida. When the bar patron had said she sat in the corner table with her dogs, I immediately pictured tiny purse-portable canines, but Rosalea's dogs were big. According to *The Pink*

Adobe Cookbook, they were served water from highball glasses and bowls of popcorn. If anyone questioned her about the dogs, she would explain they were the owners.

As for the ghost, Rosalea states, "We named the spirit that haunts the restaurant Mesera. Mesera hovers in the dining area and supplies missing lemon wedges."

As I'm leaving, Sabra points to a painting in the very center of the north wall. It's a different style than the other paintings, not so geometric and rather dark, almost brooding. "People say they can see Rosalea's face in that painting, but I don't see any face."

I examine the painting. The presence of a face is very ambiguous. Another bartender arriving for work chimes in, "I see the face right here," and he gestures at the painting. Yes, maybe so.

Sabra responds, "Somebody told me that because Rosalea was Cajun she painted her soul into that painting."

Whether she painted her soul into the picture or not, it sounds like Rosalea is still watching over her beloved Pink Adobe.

The Guadalupe Café

Connie Hernandez of the Old Santa Fe Trail Religious Articles shop advised me to look up Isabelle of the Guadalupe Café. "Some strange things have happened there," Connie told me. "You should look her up, but don't go during the rush times—Isabelle is really busy."

Heeding Connie's advice I stopped by the Guadalupe Café in mid-afternoon and it was still fairly crowded with diners, both inside and at outside patio tables under colorful umbrellas. The Guadalupe Café is just down the street from The Pink Adobe and San Miguel, and, even though I hadn't read about anything strange happening at 422 Old Santa Fe Trail, I wasn't surprised to learn of another place in the San Analco Barrio with strange things going on. The building is an old house; judging from the architectural style and detail, I'm guessing it probably dates from

The Guadalupe Café.

the 1920s or 1930s with its clay tile accents and charming arched windows.

I ask for Isabelle and after a few minutes she comes up to the front register wiping her hands and looking like any focused restaurateur interrupted in the middle of a busy day. I introduce myself, explain my mission, and that Connie Hernandez recommended I speak to her.

"Yes, yes. Here, let's sit down," she says gesturing to an empty table in the corner. She catches the eye of the cashier and says, "Find César and send him over here."

As we settle into the table, Isabelle, asks if I care for anything to drink. A handsome young man with curly hair and intense eyes who looks to be in his late teens comes up to the table and Isabelle tells him to sit down and join us.

"I was the one who experienced something first," Isabelle begins. "Well, you know how we have all these poltergeists in Santa Fe," she says as casually as if she were commenting on the Santa Fe's large number of art galleries or glitzy shops. "It

Looking out the Guadalupe Café window.

happened soon after we moved here from our former location on Guadalupe Street. I'd come in very early in the morning to bake bread and bowls would just fly off the shelves. The building had been vacant for awhile before I leased it and it seemed that something didn't like us here." Then she added, "I didn't tell any of the crew about what happened. That went on for about three months and seemed rather harmless."

Isabelle nods at the young man seated at the table. "Go ahead, César, tell her what happened to you." He takes a deep breath and says, "It was on a Sunday morning, early. I was with my dad. I came in and put my stuff down and told my dad I was going to clock in and get ready. I went down the stairs to the basement and at first I thought there was a dress, a red dress, hanging at the bottom of the stairs. I looked around and looked back and it was a woman, but I couldn't see her face. And then it was gone. I ran back up the stairs and told my dad what happened."

Isabelle adds, "I knew it had to be something real, because he didn't know anything about what I had experienced, and because he's young and hadn't experienced anything like that before. We looked all around the basement for something red, something that he might have interpreted as a red dress, but there is absolutely nothing red in the basement. We just keep supplies down there."

Cesar adds, "I couldn't go down there for the longest time. It was just too weird."

Isabelle says that she heard sage smoke might chase away ghosts, "So, I wandered around here with a burning sage stick, but *that* didn't work."

"Sometimes at night, when you're cleaning," César adds, "it's like somebody is trying to talk to you."

CANYON ROAD RESTAURANTS

Geronimo

What would the seventeenth century farmers who originally settled along the alternately dusty and muddy burro path of Canyon Road make of their winding trail to the mountains today? Their durable adobe homes with thick walls, deep-set windows, and random room arrangements have been wired for electricity and piped with modern plumbing. The floors under which they sometimes buried small children are covered with expensive tiles or wood or brick. Canyon Road, over the decades, transformed from a simple farming community to a must-see Santa Fe destination lined with galleries, shops, and eateries.

Geronimo Restaurant on Canyon Road.

East of early Santa Fe's central plaza Spanish settlers carved out small farms and coaxed crops out of the high desert soil irrigated with water diverted in acequias (ditches) from the mountains. They raised livestock and built adobe homes along the gently winding trail that is now a narrow tree-lined road, which, in true Santa Fe tradition, changes between a one and two-way street as width dictates. Since Canyon Road transformed into a world-renown art district, those once simple adobe homes, expanded often haphazardly as families grew, became "real estate" that now sells for millions through Sotheby's.

At least one farmer from those old days may be looking on in amusement and most likely amazement in the form of a ghost that makes an occasional cameo appearance in a four-star restaurant.

The restaurant Geronimo occupies one of the oldest Canyon Road homes and its name is actually a tale of two Geronimos, neither of which is the legendary Apache shaman as many people assume. Or perhaps, it's a tale of three Geronimos if you count current owner, Cliff Skoglund's, reported insistence that it's what people yell when they jump out of an airplane. The first Geronimo was Geronimo Lopez who, in 1753, began the difficult task of coaxing a farm out of the rough terrain and building a house for his family, which included thirteen children. By 1769 there were two houses on the property as well as an orchard, gardens, and pasture. Another Geronimo, Geronimo Gonzales, bought the property in 1769.

Today, Geronimo is a world-renown restaurant, where reservations are booked weeks in advance by gourmets seeking adventurous and artful food in a classic Santa Fe setting. With the exception of the decidedly un-New Mexico moose rack that graces its central fireplace, Geronimo is quintessential Santa Fe; an old adobe with charm, grace, and elegance enhanced by careful restoration and decorating.

I went to visit Geronimo after I heard a very interesting story from a person in the hospitality industry I'll call "Jason." Jason wasn't allowed to talk about the ghosts at his particular property, but he said, "I can tell you about something weird that happened to me at Geronimo." Jason says he was sitting, waiting for a table. Suddenly, in the middle of the restaurant, appeared an Hispanic man in old-fashioned dark clothes, "like from another century." The man appeared to be gazing out a window. Jason said he stared at the man, mesmerized, and couldn't believe that other diners were simply sitting and enjoying their food or conversation without noticing this strange anomaly in their midst. He said that the man started to fade away, to become transparent, "until I could see through him." At that point Jason's friends, concerned by his blank stare, started jostling him and asking him what was wrong. "I turned to them and when I turned back he was gone. I told them that there was a man standing there and he wasn't from this century. Of course people don't believe you. But, oh well."

My visit to Geronimo is in mid-afternoon just as the staff is arriving. I explain my visit to a very pleasant, friendly woman who, between answering numerous phone calls for reservations, says, yes, she's heard some people have had experiences. She takes my card and says she'll ask around. This is not a good sign for gathering ghost stories since people are understandably reluctant to call a stranger and say, "Oh, yeah. Let me tell you about the ghosts I've seen." I press her for more information and she says she has heard that the previous owner "actually saw Geronimo a number of times."

"Was he wearing old-fashioned dark clothes?" I ask.

"No, he was supposed to be in a dressing gown."

I relate the experience of the man in dark clothing appearing in the middle of the restaurant.

"Is that Jason?" she asks, smiling.

I tell her it was and she says that he had told her about the incident as well. With the phone ringing again, I thank her for her time and she assures me that she will pass my contact information along to several people at the restaurant who have had "experiences."

El Farol

For a building built in 1835 and with such a long and colorful history as Santa Fe's oldest restaurant and cantina—indeed a cantina in which a former owner was ambushed and killed as consequence of a long-standing feud—the ghosts of El Farol are remarkably well-behaved—or entertained.

Maybe it's all the lively energy and ambiance of a restaurant where the melon-colored walls are lined with colorful frescos by Alfred Morang, as well as murals and paintings swirling with the activities of dancers and musicians. Oh, and bulls. Not paintings of mean, serious bulls, but rather flamboyant, fun-loving bulls—bulls that serenade dancing senoritas with guitars; a bull playing the accordion; bulls playing sax, drum, and guitar. Or maybe it's the music every night with flamenco on Wednesdays that keeps the ghosts entertained. Or the aromas of award-winning food. And,

The bar in El Farol—the oldest bar in Santa Fe.

any bar judged "one of the best bars on earth" by the *New York Times* would likely not harbor a malicious spirit.

Whatever it is about the restaurant energy of El Farol inhabiting the old adobe building that was formerly part store, part house, it has kept ghostly activity to a relatively benign but interesting level. On my first visit I talk to a manager, Debby, who has worked at El Farol for eighteen years. She tells me she has never really experienced anything. "It's an old house," she remarks. "It breathes, it shifts around. Maybe that's what some people hear when they say they hear footsteps and see doors open and close by themselves."

Debby leads me into the cantina—a quintessential friendly old New Mexico bar with an entire wall lined with liquor bottles, cozy tables, creaky old floors—and tells me about the murder of one of the former owners near the front door. "Right here," she says. "He was stabbed right here and died. They waited until they thought he was alone. His wife tried to help and was stabbed too." Debby encourages me to contact the owner David Salazar because she knows he has more stories.

When I meet with David Salazar, he leads me to a private area in a beautiful back patio. He begins by telling me that he was born in Hernandez, a small town in northern New Mexico, and he was baptized in the church made famous by the haunting Ansel Adams photograph, "Moonrise over Hernandez." He bought the El Farol in 1985 partly because it reminded him of the home he grew up in, which was a general store on one side and a house on the other. As with many old northern New Mexico villages, it was the center of activity. Before he bought El Farol, he had never even worked at a restaurant.

In the case of El Farol, what is now the bar area was the store and the rest of the building was the home. A long portal stretches across the entire front of the building for al fresco dining in warm weather. I am amused to note that the northern New Mexico remedy for pesky flies—water-filled plastic bags—hang along the portal.

David tells me that his first introduction to ghostly activity was reports from bartenders saying that late at night there were strange sounds on the roof. "My response," he says with a hearty laugh, "was, yeah right." He said that the people working late got so spooked by the strange noises coming from the roof they refused to work alone to close up. David said he stayed late one night to help close up when the sound started. The bartender told him that was the sound they had been hearing. "I laughed and told them it was just the cat we had around the place, the cat up on the roof. Then the bartender pointed to the cat sitting in the corner and said, 'No, the cat is right there.'" David recalls the sound *did* sound like footsteps or light pounding. "And you know what's funny?" he adds. "The guys were more bothered by it than the girls. The girls could kind of take it in stride and not be bothered."

As seems to happen with many haunted places, people who worked at El Farol became accustomed to the occasional ghostly noises coming from the roof and accepted there was no reasonable explanation. David tells me that a good friend, "a famous musician, but I can't tell you his name," came to stay with him while the man was going through a difficult period in his life. The musician was intrigued by the ghosts and the next album he released had the dedication, "To the ghosts of El Farol. Thanks for the inspiration."

David says, "I want to show you something in the bar." He leads me to a fresco on the wall of a dancer defined by bright splashes of paint. It's called "Lady in Red" and Alfred Morang painted it in 1948. It's the signature picture of El Farol. David relates the story of the painting: "Supposedly there was a cocktail waitress who worked here a very long time ago. She would drink so much she could barely finish her shift. When she got drunk she would start to dance. This picture is supposed to be of her. I think this is the ghost that tap dances on the roof."

14

PROFILE
OF A GHOST HUNTER

C ody Polston is the founder and president of the Southwest Ghost Hunters Association (SGHA), an organization that conducts investigations into places where paranormal activity has been reported. Cody and his crew have investigated paranormal activity in New Mexico, Arizona, Nevada, California, Colorado, and Texas. In New Mexico alone the organization has conducted more than eighty investigations chronicled on its website, with personal accounts, photographs, and video. I find it interesting that the vast majority of places targeted are hotels and restaurants. The group has conducted a number of investigations in Santa Fe including three at the La Fonda Hotel.

I sat down with him at a trendy microbrewery in Socorro, New Mexico, where he lives, to talk to him about some of his group's investigations and to find out exactly what a ghost hunter does. We set up the meeting over the phone and I forgot to ask him what he looked like and I wasn't sure I would know who he was.

I shouldn't have worried.

He was wearing a Southwest Ghost Hunters Association t-shirt with its characteristic graphic of a fedora-crowned corpse and bandana around a skeletal neck holding a smoking six-shooter and "Southwest Ghost Hunters Association" emblazoned across

Cody Polston, founder and president of Southwest Ghost Hunters Association
Courtesy of the Southwest Ghost Hunters Association.

the front. On the back was written: "I'm a ghost hunter. If you see me running, try to keep up." The quote, Cody explains, is an inside joke since ghost hunters are often running towards the ghost instead of away from them.

I assume—wrongly—that because of his interest in ghosts he had a paranormal experience with a ghost that sparked his

(The Southwest Ghost Hunters Association logo.)

interest. "In fact," he tells me, "I was pissed because a friend of mine got ripped off by a phony psychic. I wanted to prove that all paranormal stuff was fake."

In his quest to disprove and debunk paranormal activity, he found himself in a reportedly haunted bar in Arizona. While he was sitting at the bar, some glasses floated off a shelf and dropped to the floor. He was flabbergasted. Even more astonishing was the bartender's reaction. He calmly took out a notebook and made a note of how many glasses broke. When Cody asked him what he was doing, he said he had to record the number of glasses because "it happens all the time."

"Glasses just fly off the shelves...all the time?" he asked in disbelief.

It seems the owner was keeping track of barware broken by humans as opposed to barware flung around by ghosts. Cody was so intrigued he decided to investigate paranormal activity from a more scientific standpoint, not with the goal of debunking, but simply trying to find out and quantify what happens.

Cody emphasizes that SGHA sets out to simply investigate without an agenda to prove or disprove and that investigations are conducted to test a hypothesis using the scientific method. Indeed, the SGHA website has an extensive library of reference articles like, "Applied Laws of Physics," "High Energy Particle Physics," "Field Matrix Theories," and "Quantum Bioholography." Hardly woo-woo New Age topics. Although there are topics such as "Electromagnetism for Ghost Hunters" and "Parallel Universes," the site also features "The Skeptics Corner," articles that attempt to debunk all ghostly encounters. SGHA believes those articles provide the "balance" all good ghost hunters must have.

So, it's not as if SGHA sets out to "prove" ghosts exist, but rather to understand what contributes to paranormal phenomenon and how those events can be quantified in a scientific manner, which of course "real" scientists won't do for fear of professional ridicule.

SGHA uses a variety of tools to detect electromagnetic phenomenon including an *Electronic Voice Phenomenon* device. If that seems like pseudoscience – something ghost hunters are constantly accused of – consider that no less than Thomas Edison, the most respected and resourceful inventor in America, and who, to this day, is the world record holder of patents, may have actually been working on a device to record the voices of the dead. There are some accounts that he had actually developed one. Edison is quoted in an interview in *Scientific American* as saying, "I am inclined to believe that our personality hereafter will be able to affect matter. If this reasoning be correct, then, if we can evolve an instrument so delicate as to be affected, or moved, or manipulated—whichever term you want to use—by our personality as it survives in the next life, such an instrument, when made available, ought to record something." Others have since developed recorders that tape Electronic Voice Phenomenon and these devices are a staple of professional ghost hunters along with various type of magnetic field reading devices and sophisticated photography.

When I asked Cody what a typical ghost hunt was like, he replied, "Really pretty boring. We spend a lot of time waiting for something to happen and often it never does." He laughs and says, "But there was this one time…"

It seems Cody and an associate were staking out a cemetery in Nevada where strange things happened, specifically a light, or ecotoplasmic type vapor, that could only be seen from certain angles in the deepest part of dusk before darkness. Cody's buddy was down at the bottom of a hill and Cody was as at the top; they communicated with walkie-talkies. When his buddy spotted the apparition, Cody took off at a run, to try to intercept it, the buddy giving directions over the radio.

"Suddenly, as I'm running, there is nothing under my feet. I go crashing down into a hole. Turns out it was a grave that had been eroded out from water. I'm in this eroded grave with this old coffin …"

Cody sees the horrified look on my face.

"But that's not the worst part. I hear that distinctive sound." He makes a hissing sound. "It's filled with rattlesnakes. It's a rattlesnake den. I started yelling for my buddy to help pull me out, which, fortunately, he was able to do before I got bitten."

After the rattlesnake story, we talk about the various philosophies concerning ghosts and residual human energy and we commiserate about the disdain that those who choose to explore other realms usually receive. We talk about the Santa Fe Prison and agree that it is truly a horrifying place saturated with bad energy and he tells me that it was at the prison that they had one of the most startling experiences involving lights that were not connected to electricity turning on.

As we are preparing to leave, a man approaches rather hesitantly. He looks like a rancher: worn jeans, cowboy boots, and hat. I anticipate him making a sarcastic remark about Cody's shirt or in some other way harass us. Instead, he says, "You hunt ghosts?"

Cody replies he does.

"Well, I have this problem on my ranch out by Magdelena. It's a problem with ghost riders up in a canyon. They scare the hell out of all the hands and I can't get anybody to go look for cattle up there. Especially late in the evening. I guess there were some murders on the ranch a long time ago, people are supposed to be buried in a corral."

I marvel at the unexpected twist, at how I had a preconceived misconception that a hardened cowboy would be out to ridicule a ghost hunter, not seek advice about "a problem with ghost riders." So even those of us who consider ourselves open to the unknown can have our pre-conceived misconceptions. *(Author's note: Several months later I asked Cody if SGA ever investigated the ghost riders. He laughed and said they would just add it to the huge list of future investigations to do.)*

ORBS & OTHER PHOTOGRAPHIC PHENOMENON

Once ghost stories needed no visual aids, now it seems no ghost story is credible without the requisite digital photograph of strange orbs or blurs. Cemetery shots at night seem particularly prevalent on the Internet. Photographic *anomalies* — things that show up in the picture but weren't visible to the eye — are often used as physical "evidence" of a ghostly presence or paranormal activity. Most often these anomalies are *orbs*—baffling circles of blurred light that can appear as an isolated spot or a collection of spots on a picture that sometimes look like water spots on a print. The International Ghost Hunter Society claims to have coined the term "orb" to describe these mysterious objects that appear most often in digital pictures taken at night or when a flash is used.

Most orbs are the result of natural phenomena, such as dust, pollen, or water vapor, being captured at just the right angle as to look very spooky and strange in a picture. Professional ghost hunters carefully evaluate pictures with orbs to determine if the "orb" displays *diffraction rings*—evidence that light bounced off tiny particles of dust, pollen, or water. There are the orbs that seem to glow and have no diffraction ring as well as orbs that appear in pictures that were taken without a flash. Some of these orbs can be explained by low pixel resolution digital cameras, light bouncing around from artificial sources, or the specific optics of the camera. Completely automatic small digital cameras seem particularly talented at capturing orbs or other strange blurs of light, likely because of the focal length of the lens. As some skeptics point out, there were no orbs *until* there were digital cameras while others argue that only digital cameras can actually capture disembodied energy. Indeed, some ghost hunters take the infrared chip or filter out of digital cameras in an effort to capture energy images that are supposedly more likely seen in the infrared spectrum.

There are other strange photographic phenomena such as large blurs that appear like a fog or mist. Sometimes these are referred to as *ectoplasm*—the energy residue of living beings. Again, there can be explanations related to atmosphere and camera optics. If something is obvious in the picture, why was it not obvious when the picture was taken? Think of the dust and other fine debris that is very obvious when a sunbeam slants through the window, but is completely invisible even under the brightest artificial light. You can create some of your own interesting "ghost" shots by taking a digital camera outside on a very dark night and simply snapping a picture of the darkness. The camera with all its automatic focusing and light sensing mechanisms will try to find a point to focus on and light will bounce off dust, water vapor, or even tiny insects in the air to create some very bizarre pictures.

I asked a renowned professional photographer about the strange things that appear in digital pictures. He is quick to agree that there are things of an unseen nature and admitted he has had bizarre experiences in his Chicago suburb studio that he discovered was built over an old cemetery. However, he has never captured anything unexplainable in any of the millions of photographs he's taken over his career. He explains that professional photographers set up shots and meter light carefully to get the desired effect and composition. He explains that in low light conditions, particularly with inexpensive digital cameras, the light sensing mechanisms can get confused or that light bounces around inside the camera optics to produce blurs.

I don't believe there has to be visible proof or photographic evidence to prove paranormal activity or the existence of ghosts. Those who won't or can't believe that there are things outside the realm of ordinary existence aren't going to believe pictures either.

What appear to be ghostly images at the Grant Avenue house are actually reflections.

Regardless of the reasonable, logical explanations, there *is* something very compelling and mysterious about a light or object that shows up in a picture that was not visible to the eye when the picture was taken—especially if it shows up in a place known for paranormal activity. I've had some strange things happen with my digital camera that I'd like to attribute to paranormal activity, but there's just not enough evidence. Some very odd orbs showed near the ceiling on a picture I shot through a glass door at night at the Grant Avenue house. Blowing the orbs up in Photoshop showed no diffraction rings. Still, I shot the picture at night, through glass, and there were halogen lights illuminating the room. Probably it was a strange combination of the optics and light.

Even more strange was what happened when I downloaded pictures I shot of the Oldest House into my computer. As I watched the pictures transfer from the camera to the computer I noticed one that seemed to have an interesting anomaly and I was excited to examine it more closely when the download finished. However, when the transfer was complete, everything simply vanished off my computer and off the computer memory card.

I certainly felt some strange energy when I was taking pictures in the Oldest House. Did "something" not want to be captured on film? My rational self says no, it was just a software glitch. But then, I've had other experiences with petulant spirits who have made their wishes known in most annoying ways.

15

NEW MEXICO
STATE PRISON

New Mexico State Prison.
Photo by J. B. Smith, courtesy of the New Mexico Film Office.

F ew events in New Mexico history, indeed in U.S. history,
are more grisly and disturbing than the 1980 riot at
the New Mexico State Prison in Santa Fe. No surprise

that the prison, which was closed in 1997, is haunted—indeed saturated—with the energy of angry, lost, and tortured souls. To understand this profound level of disturbing energy and the myriad reports of strange activity—including perhaps the most chilling of all Santa Fe ghost stories—it is first necessary to understand what happened at the New Mexico State Prison on the windswept Cerrillos plain just south of Santa Fe.

The riot was not the result of a brief lapse of security or random confluence of a few agitated prisoners. Indeed, prison officials had actually been warned of an impending riot on numerous occasions. The prisoner population of the New Mexico State Prison was an overturned tanker of volatile emotions leaking seething anger, festering resentments, and bitter grudges—and it had been that way for years. The emotionally incendiary conditions were the result of a prison management shaping a twisted prison society based on a "snitch system" that rewarded snitches whether the information they provided was accurate or not. In addition, the prison was chronically understaffed and the staff it did have lacked true correctional officer training and was underpaid. While a few guards had decades of experience, many were young and inexperienced—some only in their late teens. The prisoners reported that guards routinely bullied or beat them, fed a rumor mill to provoke prisoner hostilities, and generally abused their power.

Prisoners also complained bitterly about the food, but these complaints weren't the grumblings about unsavory institutional food, but rather spoiled food, like rotten green turkey served the Thanksgiving before the riot and food contaminated with rodent feces that caused illness. Following the riot, a Justice Department study found the prison to be "one of the harshest, most punitive prison environments in the nation."

With 1,136 inmates crammed in a facility designed to hold a maximum of nine hundred and other complicated social situations, it took only the tiny spark of drunken bravado to ignite an explosion of violence and carnage that sent shockwaves not only across our state but also the nation.

In the waning hours of February 1, 1980, with the glow of what the inmates called a "ghost white" full moon seeping in through the dusty windows, a small group of inmates in dormitory E-2—packed with sixty-two men—decide their stinking stash of home brew made from raisins and yeast has reached its peak of perfection and is ready for consumption. Fermented in garbage bags inside cardboard boxes, the inmates had carefully tended their stash for weeks in a pipe chase and the south wing of the prison reeked of the stuff. The inmates begin drinking heavily sometime after 10 p.m. and, emboldened by the strong liquor, they hatched a plot to jump the graveyard shift of three guards when they came around for bed check.

New Mexico State Prison.
Photo by J. B. Smith, courtesy of the New Mexico Film Office.

The graveyard shift of guards began their rounds in the early morning hours of February 2. That night there were a total of twenty-seven guards on duty, but only fifteen of them are actually inside the prison. In dormitory E-2 an inmate jumps an eighteen year-old guard. Other inmates watch transfixed as the guard struggles, but is quickly over-powered. That defeat of power charges up the dormitory and inmates leap from their bunks and overpower the other two guards. Incredibly, the guards had not locked the dormitory door behind them, but rather left it ajar. When the overpowered guards are not immediately rescued by other guards in the facility, the residents of E-2 spill out of the dormitory, armed with shanks and ax handles, and fueled with strong liquor and years of pent-up rage.

Not only is the door to the dormitory not locked, the grilles inside the prison designed to compartmentalize any potential violence are not deployed. Indeed, they were seldom ever used and the inmates knew that. In the ensuing melee, guards lost their keys—keys that would open almost all the doors in the prison. Quickly inmates seized the prison's control center, shattering the highly touted bullet-resistant glass in a new control center by throwing a fire extinguisher through it. Less than half an hour later, the inmates controlled the entire prison and were bragging about it over the guards' two-way radios to the outside world.

Twelve guards are taken hostage. Two guards hide in a tiny crawl space and endure thirty-six harrowing hours in the cold and damp, but are never found. A medical technician manages to barricade himself and seven invalid inmates in an infirmary and they too are overlooked by the rioters. The inmates begin setting fires and ripping apart plumbing to flood what isn't burning. An assistant warden, roused at his residence, orders guards in the towers to arm themselves and shoot anyone who runs to the perimeter. The State Police are summoned. The assistant warden's family is evacuated from the grounds.

The most dangerous and violent prisoners are released from Cell Block 3 by the first group of rioters using the guards' keys and by accessing an electronic control panel with operations that are familiar because the inmates have carefully observed its workings many times. Inmates break into the pharmacy and begin ingesting the massive quantities of drugs stored there. With bandannas as tourniquets, they begin shooting up all the liquid drugs they can find. Other inmates break into the basement shops where they can sniff paint and glue.

Chaos reigns.

The State Police surround the penitentiary and the inmates inform them via two-way radio that they will kill the guards if there is any attempt to retake the prison. The State Police are joined by SWAT teams and then the National Guard.

At first the rampage is generalized and directed at the prison infrastructure and inanimate objects, but then it becomes focused on hated human targets: snitches.

The first mark is a young thief from the northern New Mexico village of Chimayo, the village of mystical events and miraculous healing earth. The residents of Chimayo didn't take kindly to a thief who stole from his neighbors in the tight knit community. With no town police, the neighbors tried repeatedly to capture the young man. He eluded capture—both by the townspeople and the county sheriff—so often a village legend developed that he was a shape-shifter capable of turning himself into a dog and sneaking off undetected through the brush. Or, that he was half boy, half dog. Because of this strange skill he became known as the Dog Boy of Chimayo. Eventually whatever bizarre talent or mystical ability he had to elude detection failed him and he was captured and sent to prison. He even tried to escape from prison—twice. But again, he wasn't able to summon his old abilities, was eventually recaptured, and only succeeded in netting himself more time.

The Dog Boy of Chimayo also had another moniker—one that would prove fatal: "King of the snitches." Dog Boy was confined in the "Hole" for throwing coffee on a guard. The "Hole," located in the basement beneath Cell Block 3, is an isolated solitary confinement cell where prisoners are locked naked behind a solid steel door with only a thin mattress on a concrete bench. The prisoners come for Dog Boy in the "Hole" with an acetylene torch. His first reaction is arrogance and bravado, but when the torch continues to hiss and the door gets warmer, Dog Boy's bluster turns to pleaded negotiation, insistence that he hadn't snitched.

Next, he was begging for his life.

When the inmates finally cut through the steel door, they dragged Dog Boy upstairs to Cellblock 3 as he screams, "*No era yo, no lo hice*" (It wasn't me. I didn't do it.). The rioters intend to make a spectacle of him. Of all the horrific tortures that would take place during the course of the riot, Dog Boy endured perhaps the worst, eventually begging his captors to kill him and put him out of his misery since it seemed as if his body refused to die as he was beset with increasingly vicious and cruel torture.

When Dog Boy did eventually die, inmates, stoked with blood lust, drugs, and revenge, descended on Cell Block 4, the "protective custody" unit housing the snitches. But Cell Block 4 didn't just house snitches—it was also where the weak, the child molesters and murderers, and the mentally ill resided—the very mentally ill for whom there was no other secure facility in New Mexico except prison. There were also parole violators and prisoners who would later be identified by the state medical examiner as having refused to pay kickbacks to guards.

In the early moments of the riot, one guard had managed to radio to the guard stationed near Cell Block 4 to lower the protective grille. All ninety-six men in Cell Block 4 are locked in cells as they watch potential torturers tediously burn through the grille barrier with acetylene torches. After several hours of listening to the ominous sizzle of torches and hearing death taunts, the inmates of Cell Block 4 see lights flashing on the walls. Located on the northwest corner of the prison, the cellblock is close to both the perimeter fence and a sally port, a double gated access directly into the prison yard. What the prisoners see is the light of State Police cars and other vehicles pulling up along the fence and they suppose it to be a beacon of salvation. Believing they will be rescued, the inmates flash SOS with lights and scream desperately for help. One inmate survivor would later report, "I mean all the state troopers were right there. They were parked all up and down the fence, man. You could see them driving inside the sally port. Why didn't they come in? The door was *right there*."

Via radio transmission to the outside, the rioters make clear that when they breach Cell Block 4 there will be a massacre. While authorities could have used duplicate keys or the prison locksmith to open the back door, which indeed was *right there*, they insisted in later testimony they did nothing to save the prisoners in Cell Block 4 for fear the hostages would be killed. At dawn, as the crazed inmates, carrying years of grudges, have nearly burned through the grille, there is the desperate realization by the inmates in Cell Block 4 that there will be no rescue mission. The prisoners resort to pathetic means to try to secure themselves in their cells, tying bed sheets and towels around the doors and barricading the doors with bunks. Eventually, in the early morning hours, the inmates break through the grille.

Torture and carnage reign.

Some inmates are spared, sometimes only because their cell doors malfunctioned and wouldn't open. Some escape in the maelstrom of chaos. As the prisoners eventually leave the area littered with bodies, blood, and feces, a corpse spasms and sits up. Despite all they've done *this* horrifies the prisoners. Interpreting it as an omen, they beat it down.

Writing in *The Devil's Butcher Shop*, Roger Morris, breaking from his brutally factual and gripping journalistic prose, states: "For months to come, old inmates and new will feel ghosts in 4, describe pockets of chill air, and sounds in their cells at dawn."

Early on in the uprising, eighty inmates who wanted no part of it flee to the prison baseball field. They would be joined by one hundred more horrified survivors seeking refuge by the fence where, by early morning, the National Guard, in full combat gear and bearing bayonet tipped M-16s, will be stationed. Remarkably, there is no single person communicating the demands of the prisoners, nor is there a single State official responsible for attempting to negotiate the release of the hostages. A variety of prisoners insist they just want a press conference to air their grievances about conditions in the prison.

As the riot grinds on hour after bloody hour, there are noble acts and heroics among men many average citizens believe to have no morals or ethics; heroics that saved lives, sometimes resulting in the death of the rescuer. Inmate medics ministered to the severely injured and overdosed and struggled to keep the brutalized guards alive. Inmates protect the three guards considered "decent men," secreting them through the smoke past rioters to different locations. A group of inmates uses an acetylene torch to help wounded survivors of Cell Block 4 escape out an exterior door in Cell Block 5 where they are taken by helicopter and ambulance to Santa Fe's St. Vincent Hospital. And there is the desperate appeal of an inmate leader pleading over the prison radio band: "Attention all units. Attention all units. Stop killing each other, stop killing each other. I repeat. No more killing. No more hurting each other." There's a long pause and, he finishes, "Man, there's blood all over this damn floor...up to your ankles."

As reported in the *Albuquerque Journal*, "When State Police marched into the Penitentiary of New Mexico on February 3, 1980, they didn't retake the prison from rioting inmates so much as they occupied the charred shell after the riot had burned itself out."

The State Police or National Guard **NEVER** fired a shot.

When it was over thirty-three inmates were killed, most in unspeakably brutal ways after first being tortured. However, some died of drug overdoses. Even the death toll is disputed because of the horrific fires that may have incinerated more and because the last official population tally was on a control center grease board that was destroyed. Estimates of prisoner injuries and drug overdoses were at more than one hundred, overwhelming Santa Fe's St. Vincent Hospital. Of the guards taken hostage, none were killed though some were physically and sexually brutalized. It was, and remains, the second most deadly prison riot in United States history, after the Attica Prison Riot of 1971.

Bodies and what remained of bodies were loaded into trucks and ambulances and removed from the prison. And, most chilling of all, when the ambulance with the remains of the Dog Boy of Chimayo passed the row of patrol cars marked K-9 with the highly disciplined police dogs quietly waiting to be deployed, the dogs, one by one, began to bark and howl, refusing to be quieted by their handlers.

According to an assessment of the aftermath, two dormitories and the gymnasium were burned-out shells. The administrative offices, the psychiatric unit, and the education wing were destroyed. Nearly every mattress was burned. The Protestant chapel was demolished, but the Catholic chapel, with the exception of blood from a brutal murder in the aisle, was unmarred. Some prisoners were sent to out-of-state facilities while the prison was repaired, but many remained as the prison simply carried on its operation amidst the wreckage.

When Governor Bruce King, noted for his malapropisms, was asked by reporter Sam Donaldson about long-standing rumors that there would be a riot, he replied that speculating about that issue would "open up a whole box of Pandoras."

The numerous problems of the prison were not resolved even after public outcry and official inquiry and, in the years before it was eventually shut down to be replaced by a new prison nearby, several guards and a number of inmates were killed.

Today the prison, referred to as Old Main, is used by movie and television productions as part of the state's incentive to attract the entertainment industry to New Mexico. The large buildings are used for set construction and the sprawling complex for vehicle and equipment storage, and as a staging area for crews. Several movies have been filmed at the prison; a low-budget horror movie and a 2005 remake of the comedy, "The Longest Yard." A frequently repeated story relates that before filming of "The Longest Yard," star Adam Sandler had a priest, a rabbi, and a shaman perform a blessing ceremony at the prison because of the disturbing energy it exuded.

I have been to the prison once and I was startled by what a troubling experience it was. I went to the prison to assess the damage to my vintage Airstream travel trailer that I had rented to a movie for use as a set prop. The Airstream was damaged by a pyrotechnic stunt gone awry and hauled to the prison for storage. Because the Airstream was located in an out of the way nook, it took considerable driving around and searching for it in the sprawling compound. While some parts of the prison have just the generally creepy, depressing look of a Dickens orphanage or abandoned Rust-belt industrial building, other structures seem to ooze a terrifying energy.

I had not expected the prison to have such the profound impact on me that it did. The riot had happened a very long time ago, and the prison had been closed for nearly a decade. Like most New Mexicans I had watched the news accounts of the prison riot with an uncomprehending bewilderment and horror. While the networks announced that they were showing only the least disturbing images, I remember that even many of those were too horrible to watch and I looked away.

I had expected that my concern over my beloved Airstream would greatly outweigh any weirdness of the place. When I finally found my Airstream and got out to survey the damage, I had the distinct and very unsettling feeling of being watched. But not just watched...visually stalked by unseen eyes. I looked up at the blank and broken out windows, but saw nothing. *There was just a feeling...*

Even though the prison was the site of bustling movie activity just like a Hollywood back lot with trucks coming and going and hammering and sawing as pieces of large sets were being erected, there was something indefinable about it, a low-level malevolence...as if the vacant windows were crowded with angry, peering eyes. I was as distressed by the visit as I was by the damage to my Airstream and, while I initially had no objections to it being stored at the prison until repairs could be arranged, I wanted it out of there immediately.

Apparently the feeling of being watched or followed is not uncommon. A number of set-builders working on various movies in the various prison buildings reported the same experience: they felt like they were being watched or followed. One woman associated with a state program said that she had been in the prison many times with groups of people and felt nothing unusual. However, on one occasion she found herself alone in a hall and felt a wave of inexplicable fear. There were also reports among movie workers of a hospital gurney that had been in the basement mysteriously showing up in main hallways and moving by itself.

††††††††††††††

From the disturbing level of my daytime experience at the prison, as well as those of movie workers, it seems almost incomprehensible to visit there at night, but that is just what Southwest Ghost Hunters Association did in 2002. SGHA identified several areas on which to focus their investigations.

Their account states:

> "The most active areas of the prison are Cell Blocks 3 and 4, the tool room, and the laundry room. Cell Block 3 was the maximum-security ward that also contained the solitary confinement cell. Activity reported here includes unexplainable noises, doors that open and close by themselves, and lights that turn on and off without any apparent cause.
>
> "Cell block 4 was the area where the "snitches" and other prisoners held in protective custody were contained. Upon entering the cellblock, there are marks on the floor where rioters used power

tools to decapitate the snitches and several other inmates. Also visible are the outlines of scorch marks where other inmates were burned to death with propane cutting torches. Another inmate was hung from the upper tier of the cellblock with sheets that had been tied together. The activity reported here is similar to those reported in Cell Block 3. Twenty-three of the inmates who were murdered during the riot were killed in Cell Block 4.

"The laundry room was the site of several murders, although they occurred long before the riot of 1980. It is located in a labyrinth of corridors that lie underneath the prison. These corridors also link to the gas chamber, many mechanical rooms, and the tool room, where the inmates stole the propane torches and other tools that were used during the riots. Uneasy feelings and whispers are often reported down there as well as unusual human shaped shadows."

SGHA's 2002 expedition was done as part of a promotion with a local radio station just before Halloween. Professional ghost hunters sometimes conduct such promotional-type hunts to both gain publicity and funds to buy expensive equipment. The radio station chose contestants for a "dare" type of contest in which a person had to go alone into a particularly terrifying part of the prison and stay there for twenty minutes. Here's what happened to the ghost hunters before the contest even began:

"After arriving at the prison, we were briefed on the contest and that there was a "holding area near the front entrance where everyone would wait while the contestants did their "dares." We were then given a tour of the grounds, including Cell Block 4 and the basement. The contestants were not due to arrive for another hour and a half, giving us a chance to take some initial readings for unusual electromagnetic fields.

"After the tour we took IR [infrared] cameras down to solitary confinement in Cell Block 3 to monitor the contestant there, to ensure that he stayed in the cell for the full twenty minutes of his 'dare.' After we positioned the camera, Cody moved to the far end of the corridor to take photographs while Bob shot IR video from the other end. After a few minutes there was a distinct sound of a cell door slowly opening or closing. As Cody moved towards the area where the sound seemed to be coming from, a second similar noise, this time much louder and faster, echoed down the hallway behind Cody's position.

Bob, assuming that the noise was coming from the contestants, started to radio into the holding area to confirm that the contestants had arrived. Suddenly his radio started changing frequencies by itself and a [sic] extremely loud noise echoed down the hallway that resembled a cell door violently slamming shut. The sound came from somewhere behind Cody, who had moved forward to look for the source of the first strange noise.

Bob quickly moved forward towards Cody's position and after verifying that he was okay, began checking the area. All of the cell doors were closed and locked when we arrived to set up the cameras and they were still locked. We attempted to replicate the sound by opening and closing several doors that were unlocked and by banging on the cell doors themselves. However, we could not replicate anything that sounded close to the noises we heard earlier.

"After trying unsuccessfully to replicate the sound in Cell Block 3's basement, we moved up two levels to the top tier. We discover a rather strange EM [electromagnetic] field near the far side of the cellblock in the last cell on that row. The field was 5 nanotesla and had an originating point directly in the center of the cell. We were not able to determine exactly what was causing this field.

"We continued down the catwalk of the cellblock, taking photos and readings. Just as we reached the end of the catwalk, a repeating thumping noise moved across a ventilation pipe towards us, eventually stopping three feet away from our position. Although it was quite strange and downright spooky, we assumed it was a wild animal running inside of the pipe towards us. We then moved back to the holding area at the front of the prison to take a break.

"Once we were outside, we were able to talk to some of the former guards of the prison and showed the video of the incident in Cell Block 3 to them and the radio staff. One of the guards thought the sound resembled a fuse blowing out down there and went to check it out. Meanwhile, several of the radio staff had heard noises coming from the guard tower while we were in Cell Block 3. They said that the noises sounded like the trap door of the guard tower being opened and slammed shut. So we all moved off to the tower to check it out.

"Bob immediately picked up on a very strong D/C electromagnetic field near the tower. The readings fluctuated between 2 to 8 nanotesla, DC. As he moved about, trying to isolate the origin of the field, the remainder of the group received visitors, one being the former warden of the prison. When asked about the tower and if anything had happened there, he simply replied, "There are some things you just do not want to know." He would not comment on the tower any further. Bob continued measuring the D/C field by the tower while Cody took photographs. Shortly afterwards, the contestants arrived and the contest began.

"While waiting during the contest, the guard who checked the fuses in Cell Block 3 returned and informed us that the fuses were all okay. He had no idea what could have caused that noise. After the completion of the "dare" in Cell Block 4, we were able to move around that area and see what we could find. We were on the bottom tier walking towards the opposite end of the corridor when the squeaky sound of a metal door closing rang out from behind us. We turned to see that one of the doors we had passed was wide open. We moved to check out that area, but found nothing unusual with our instruments. The door itself was quite heavy, maybe sixty pounds or so, and the hinges were rusted. After manually closing and opening it, we ruled out the possibility of it being pushed open by a gust of air or by the vibration of us walking past it. We later learned from a guard that all of these doors had been locked. The door that had opened was very freaky because it was locked shut and they did not have a key for it, making it impossible to even open it in the first place."

SGHA Conclusions:

"In addition to the video and EVP [electronic voice phenomenon] samples collected at the penitentiary, two interesting photographs were obtained as well.

"Despite the fact that the electricity had been shut off, a light in Cell Block 3 remained on. When checked, there was no voltage flowing through the power line to that light bulb."

Contestant Experiences

The radio station selected five people to perform a variety of "dares" in the parts of the prison considered to be the most terrifying such as the mental ward and the gas chamber. One of the locations was "the Hole." In addition, one contest was to attempt to communicate with ghosts via an ouija board on the spot where prisoners were beheaded with power tools. Contestants were randomly teamed up with radio station DJs who would lead them to their challenge area and then return twenty minutes later to "rescue" them, returning with them to the "safe" area where they would recount their experiences. If the contestants became too frightened to continue with their dare, they were to yell "uncle!" and their teammate would immediately return with the flashlight.

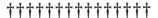

The first contestant, Rich, was paired with DJ Rainman. Rich drew the "Hole" and was escorted to it by Rainman who took his flashlight, leaving him in absolute darkness. Rainman warns Rich not to close the door because "we won't be able to get it open."

Rich completed his entire twenty-minute dare. When Rainman returned and asked him, "How's it goin'?" Rich replied, "I'm freaked man, psyched."

Rainman asked Rich if he was OK and he replied yes, adding, "I'm freaked. I'm psyched, but I'm fine. It was freaky man, I heard all kinds of noises and s--t." He then asked Rainman, "Is [sic] there dogs here?"

"Dogs?" Rainman asks. "I think there are some, uh a lot of wild animals living here," he adds.

"Because it sounded like barking or howling or something," Rich replies. "I was like, what?"

"Coming from in here?" Rainman asks.

"Yeah!" Rich replies. After Rainman presents him with his flashlight, Rich proclaims, "That was freaky brother, freaky!"

Barking dogs.

Not far away voices, crying, groaning, or singing, no sounds of movement or footsteps or other more typical paranormal audio phenomenon. Barking dogs. In "the Hole"—the place the Dog Boy of Chimayo drew his last breaths before being tortured—barking dogs, just like when Dog Boy's body passed the K-9 units outside the prison. In addition, despite what Rainman said, it *is* unlikely that animals as big as dogs would actually be living inside the fenced prison grounds, much less inside the prison itself.

As Rich and Rainman make their way back to the "safe zone," a light startles them.

"That light is **not** supposed to be on," Rainman says. "The power is cut off to this building."

The next contestant is Hollie, who is teamed with DJ TJ Trout. Her assignment is to be strapped to a bed in the most remote cell in the mental ward. TJ Trout instructs Hollie that if she sees anything or hears anything, "I want you to talk to it. I want you to ask it questions."

When TJ Trout returns at the end of twenty minutes, Hollie seems surprised that her dare is over so quickly. She reports that she heard a far away crying sound and that she saw lights flashing through the window. "There's no electricity, right?" she asks.

"No electricity." TJ confirms. Then he asks, "But you had no opportunity to talk to anybody?"

"No, it [the crying] was like faint and far away."

As TJ frees Hollie from her restraints, she says, "You know what's weird though? My right hand is way colder than anything else on my body…Maybe someone came and held my hand."

As they left the area, TJ tells Hollie, "Yeah, the guards said, 'They'll be different with female energy in there. They'll go crazy with female energy.'"

Contestant Chevon, paired with DJ Mahoney, proceeds to the gas chamber. Mahoney emphasizes, "We're not going to do anything to try to scare you. If you hear anything, we're not doing it. We are truly letting whatever happens, happen."

When Mahoney returns, Chevon exclaims, "Am I done?"

Joking, Mahoney replies, "No, that was only four minutes."

"Man, there were some freaky noises. I was scared."

"But, you didn't yell 'uncle.'"

"No, but it was like somebody was behind me dragging like a chair. You could hear metal scraping across the ground. And it stopped right behind me. It was consistent. There was this [makes scraping sound] and it would stop. And then a few seconds later [makes scraping sound]. You could hear it start over by the door and slide behind me."

"Ok, I'll yell 'Uncle' if you don't," Mahoney says with a laugh.

The final challenge pairs Maggie with DJ Swami. With candles, an ouija board, and a list of questions, Maggie is supposed to sit on the floor next to the beheading marks and try to summon a spirit. She brings with her offerings for the spirits: cigarettes, matches and a 40-ounce can of Schlitz beer.

"I'm not here to judge you," Maggie begins, "I have brought you gifts. Uh...I already opened the beer. Sorry. First question. Are you with us?"

Silence.

"How did you die?" Maggie asks.

Without leaving much time for contemplation, Maggie asks, "Is there anything you'd like to tell me that you did not get to say before you died?"

Silence.

"Are you alone or are there others with you?" She pauses and then asks in rapid succession, "Will you give me a sign that you are present? Will you speak to me? Will you show yourself to me?"

There is a brief pause and then Maggie announces, "I'm done."

When Swami comes for her, Maggie, disappointed, proclaims, "Nothing happened. My ouija board didn't move. They didn't come smoke or drink with me."

The fact that Maggie received no response from the ouija board is not surprising considering that, perhaps due to the general creepiness and situation, and the fact that she was a contestant who just had to make it through her gig to qualify for some sort of prize, she hurried through the entire process rather than giving the standard one to five minutes response time most ouija board experts recommend. In addition, ouija boards are supposed to be used by two people, preferably a man and a woman, and some experts recommend a third person, a scribe, to record the movements for later analysis.

Radio station publicity stunts aside, the Santa Fe's New Mexico State Prison is a profoundly haunted place and remains so to this day. While any abandoned prison with all the energies associated with incarceration would likely be haunted, the lingering residue of riot terror puts this prison in a dimension by itself.

16

LA LLORONA

No book about Santa Fe ghosts would be complete without the story of La Llorona (lah yoh-ROH-nah). Variously called the wailing woman, the weeping woman, or the woman in white, La Llorona roams near the water, crying over her drowned children. There are many versions of the ancient Latin American legend. Indeed, La Llorona is an archetypal tale with variations in many cultures around the world. The common themes are a vengeful or despondent woman crying or wailing near bodies of water because she has killed her children. Other elements of the story may include a man of higher social standing than the wailing woman who has betrayed her, seduction of men by the wailing woman, or the wailing woman as a harbinger of death.

In Greek myth she is Medea, a sorceress who marries the noble hero Jason, bears two sons and, when Jason leaves her for another, murders the sons and sends Jason's new love interest poison.

Some African tribes tell the story of the wind as a wailing woman searching along the waterways for her children, murdered by the ocean that, then, scattered the children's remains throughout the world.

In Slavic legend, she is a *rusalka*, a female water spirit. A *rusalka* comes into being if a young woman is drowned by a lover in a lake or when unbaptized children born out of wedlock are drowned by their mothers.

Lilith, in Jewish folklore, was the disobedient first wife of Adam who was cast out as a demon and, in some versions of the tale, ate babies at night or led young men and women astray.

The origin of the La Llorona story in New Mexico likely originated through a combination of stories related to the Spanish conquest of Mexico. Around 1500 the Aztec goddess Cihuacoatl was said to appear in white, weeping for her lost children, saying, "Oh my children, where can I take you?" This appearance was believed to be an omen to the indigenous people regarding the arrival of Hernán Cortés. However the dominant story of the many variations on the legend identifies La Llorona as Malinche.

According to the most well-defined version of the story of Malinche/La Llorona a girl is born into Aztec nobility around 1505. She is sold to a Mayan merchant as a slave and learns Mayan in addition to her native Nahuatl. Because of her linguistic abilities in the two primary indigenous languages of Mexico, Malinche becomes an interpreter for Hernán Cortés and also his lover. She gives birth to twin boys by Cortés.

Because of his significant conquests, the Spanish king and queen believe Cortés is conspiring to build his own empire and recall him to Spain. Cortés refuses, fearing the newly conquered people will rebel in his absence. A beautiful woman is sent by Spanish royalty to woe him and convince him to return to Spain.

Cortés falls in love with the Spanish woman and tells Malinche he will be taking their children and returning to Spain. Realizing that she betrayed her people only to be betrayed by Cortés, Malinche prays to her gods and in a vision receives a message that if Cortés takes the boys, one will return to Mexico and complete the slaughter of her people.

Malinche flees with her boys, but as Cortés' soldiers close in on her, she pulls a dagger, stabs her babies, and drops them in Lake Tenochtitlan, screaming, "Oh, hijos mios!" (My children!)

A letter in the Spanish archives written by Cortés states: "After God, we owe the conquest of New Spain to Doña Marina (Malinche)." In contrast to her praise by the Spanish, in Mexico "Malinche" becomes another word for betrayal and is often preceded by "La" (the).

The first documented appearances of La Llorona occurred in 1550 after the death of La Malinche. She would appear on the night of the full moon wearing a white dress and a veil over her face and crying before she vanished in the lake.

All of the small Hispanic villages in New Mexico tell stories that are a variation on the theme of La Llorona, sometimes updated with modern details to make them less like a folktale and more like the Latino version of soap operas, *telenovelas*. The La Llorona tale serves a useful purpose for parents in helping keep children away from water. It's one thing to simply warn children to stay away from the river or *acequia* (irrigation ditch) and quite another thing to tell them that if they get too close to the water La Llorona will take them.

There are number of tales of La Llorona encounters in Santa Fe. One story tells of a man listening to a police band on his shortwave radio late one night in the 1980s. A woman called the police to report that La Llorona was crying down by the Santa Fe River. In other cities such a report would not be taken seriously. However, in Santa Fe, La Llorona *is* taken seriously—in this case even by the police. Five cruisers were dispatched to the area. The man listening to the radio traffic on his shortwave radio said the police would hear crying over by a tree and sneak up on it... only to find nothing. The radio chatter of the officers described the sound as it moved around and some officers stated it sounded like a baby crying. After half an hour of chasing the crying sound, one officer conceded that since it was La Llorona she would never be found and they left.

One particularly fascinating old story concerned an encounter with a presence perceived to be La Llorona by a family traveling by covered wagon who witnessed the apparition in a rural area east of Santa Fe. In rural New Mexico such transportation was common as late as the early 1900s.

The family had been traveling through a summer downpour. When the rain finally let up, they decided to stop and eat. As they were sitting outside their wagon enjoying the fragrant air and the astonishing play of light from the shifting clouds and rain-spangled trees, they spotted a woman galloping a white horse off in the distance. The woman headed toward them, her *tapalo* (shawl) blowing across her face and out behind her. Because La Llorona is said to sometimes ride a white horse, the family jumped in the wagon and held the flaps closed for they knew that what they saw was *un aparación de el otro mundo*—something from another world. They heard the woman approach the wagon and dismount. Huddled in terrified silence, they listened as she slowly circled their wagon as if inspecting it. Even after they heard her remount and ride off, the family sat quietly in the wagon, waiting to make sure it was safe. When they finally climbed out, they saw the footprints of the woman in the damp sand, but none for her horse. They walked for a distance from the wagon looking for evidence of a galloping horse and there was none.

In several more contemporary Santa Fe La Llorona stories, she appears in miniature form. In one instance a man was walking home from a bar on Good Friday along Acequia Madre (the mother ditch) Road. He saw a woman dressed all in white in the moonlight. The woman pointed a long bony finger at him. He started running in fear. When he reached his own driveway he was startled to find a crying baby in the middle of it. He picked up the baby and pulled the blanket away from its face to reveal a tiny La Llorona with pointed teeth and dark, sunken eyes. The baby-sized La Llorona pointed a bony finger at him.

He dropped the baby and ran into his house and swore off drinking forever.

The other miniature La Llorona appeared to a movie projectionist for Santa Fe's old Paris Theater who was riding his bicycle home late one night in 1949. He came upon a tiny woman, less then four feet tall who began to make a terrible moaning and crying sound as soon as she saw him. The crying rose to a terrible scream. The man dropped his bicycle and took off running to escape the sound of her terrifying cry.

There are a number of other stories of La Llorona, some bordering on urban legend type stories and several focused on encounters with La Llorona by drunks, one of whom claimed La Llorona beat him up and threw him in the Santa Fe River.

Like many Hispanics in rural northern New Mexico, Bernadine Santisteven grew up hearing stories of La Llorona as the woman who drowned her children in revenge for an unfaithful lover and was condemned to roam waterways crying in anguish. The stories, which she at first believed were unique to her town, both terrified and fascinated her and she decided to explore the legend in depth. Beginning in 1998, for the next five years Bernadine searched for stories of La Llorona. She discovered that stories of La Llorona were told all over Latin America. In addition to collecting music, poems, and artwork dedicated to La Llorona, Bernadine interviewed people who claimed to have had encounters with La Llorona, either seeing her or hearing her. She worked with historians and Jungian psychologists who studied La Llorona as a female archetype and discovered stories similar to La Llorona were told worldwide. She started a website for people to share their experiences. Bernadine was also interested in the contemporary tragedies of American women who drowned their children such as Susan Smith of South Caroline in 1995, Andrea Yates of Texas in 2001, and Bernadine Flores, who drowned herself and her two children in a river near Pilar in northern New Mexico in 2002.

After five years of research Bernadine felt she knew La Llorona well enough to write a screenplay about her. She quit her job as a venture capitalist in New York City to fulfill her dream of creating "The Cry," a contemporary supernatural thriller based on the legend of La Llorona that would be shot in New Mexico and New York City.

There were several strange events during the production of "The Cry" that almost seem orchestrated by La Llorona herself. First, just days before shooting was scheduled to begin on a river location Bernadine chose in northern New Mexico—a scene in which La Llorona drowns her child—Bernadine discovered that two years earlier, at that exact same location, a woman named Bernadine Flores drowned her two children and herself.

In dialog of "The Cry," La Llorona states: "Sisters. You're like me. You're fingers will scrape the bottom of the rivers searching for your child and you will cry tears of blood." While at work on post-production of "The Cry," post-production manger Claudia experienced a freak medical condition in which tears of blood dripped out of her eyes.

There's no doubt about the deep connection of La Llorona to Santa Fe. When Bernadine Santisteven held a test screening in Santa Fe of the near-complete version of "The Cry," nearly 2,000 people waited in line for hours in hopes of being able to see it.

During an audio interview on her website, Bernadine remarked on her relationship with La Llorona. "After growing up with La Llorona and searching for her all these years, I think I know her pretty well. And even though I'm not afraid of her anymore, I am more certain of one thing than I ever was before: La Llorona is real."

17

THE DRIVING "GHOST"

This is a story from Northern New Mexico. Everyone who tells it swears it is true. It happened near Espanola, north of Santa Fe, and it starts like many a good ghost story should...

It was a dark and stormy night.

A man was hitchhiking from Velarde to Espanola, but no cars went by. The storm was so strong, the man could hardly see a few feet ahead of him. Suddenly, there in San Juan, he saw a car slowly coming toward him.

It stopped.

The man was so tired and wet that, when the car stopped, he got in without looking and closed the door. Before he could say "Thank you," he realized that there was nobody behind the wheel.

The car started off very slowly. The man looks at the road ahead and sees a curve. He starts to pray and begs for his life. Just before the car goes over the edge, a hand appears through the window and turns the wheel.

By then the man is paralyzed with terror. He watches as the hand appears each time the car approaches a curve. Gathering his courage, he jumps out of the car and runs all the way to Ranchitos.

Wet and in shock, he goes into Red's, asks for two shots of tequila, and, crying hysterically, starts telling everybody about his terrifying experience.

About a half hour later, two men walk into Red's and one says to the other, "Mira, Jose! That's the pendejo that got in the car while we were pushing it!"

Bibliography

Auslander, Jason. "'Ghost' Keeps People Guessing." *Santa Fe New Mexican*, June 16, 2007.

Beatty, Judith. *La Llorona: Encounters With the Weeping Woman*. Santa Fe, New Mexico: Sunstone Press, 2004.

Bernadine Santistevan, creator of www.lallorona.com and co-writer, director, and producer of "The Cry."

Brochure, "San Miguel"

Brochure, "The Oldest House"

Carney, Cary. *Native American Higher Education in the United States*. Edison, New Jersey: Transaction Books, 1999.

Gallagher, Mike. "1980 prison riot a black mark on state's history." *Albuquerque Journal*, September 19, 1999.

Haining, Peter. *Dictionary of Ghosts*. Robert Hzle, London or Trafalgar, Chicago: 1999.

Hirliman, Georgelle. *The Hate Factory: A First-hand Account of the 1980 Riot at the Penitentiary*. iUniverse, Inc., 2005.

Hudnall, Ken. *Spirits of the Border IV: The History and Mystery of New Mexico*. Rhinebeck, New York: Omega Press, 2005.

Mayer, Robert. *Notes of a Baseball Dreamer: A Memoir*. Chicago, Illinois: Houghton/Mifflin, 2003.

McGeagh, Robert. *Juan de Onate's Colony in the Wilderness: An Early History of the American Southwest*. Santa Fe, New Mexico: Sunstone Press, 1990.

Morris, Roger. *The Devil's Butcher Shop, The New Mexico Prison Uprising*. Albuquerque, New Mexico: University of New Mexico Press, 1983.

Murphy, Rosalea. *The Pink Adobe Cookbook*. New York, New York: Dell, 1988.

New Mexico Tourism website.

Norman, Michael. *Haunted Heritage: A Definitive Collection of North American Ghost Stories*. New York, New York: Tor Books, 2003.

Nuccetelli, Susana, editor. *Can the Dead Speak? Forthcoming in Themes from G. E. Moore: New Essays in Epistemology and Ethics*. Oxford, United Kingdom: Oxford University Press.

Ortiz, Yvette and James Clark, Larisa Gomez, Luis Cortinas and Ruben Cam. "Oñate Conquered Desert to Explore Southwest." *Borderlands: an El Paso Community College Local History Project,* January 2008.

Pratt. R. H. *Battlefield and Classroom: Four decades with the American Indian, 1867-1904*. Norman, Oklahoma: University of Oklahoma Press.

Randall, Guy. "Ghosts of San Miguel." *Santa Fe Arts and Culture Magazine*, September 6, 2007.

Roberts, David. *The Pueblo Revolt: The Secret Rebellion That Drove the Spaniards Out of the Southwest*. New York, New York: Simon and Schuster, 2004.

"Soul Wound: The Legacy of Native American Schools." *Amnesty Magazine*, Summer 2003. (http://www.amnestyusa.org/amnestynow/soulwound.html)

"The Inexplicable Stairs: Answer to a Prayer to St. Joseph." *St. Joseph Magazine*, April 1960.

Wallace, David. *Education for Extinction - American Indians and the Boarding School Experience 1875-1928*. Lawrence, Kansas: Adams University Press of Kansas, 1995.

Weideman, Paul. "San Miguel a Jewel of the Old Barrio." *Santa Fe Real Estate*, May, 2008.

Wikipedia. Rod Cell: Citation to Kandel E.R., Schwartz, J.H., Jessell, T.M. *Principles of Neural Science*, 4th Ed. New York, New York: McGraw-Hill, 2000.

Internet Sources

http://www.abba.com/b/769

http://www.archdiocesesantafe.org/AboutASF/Chimayo.html

http://dartmouth.edu/~rasoren/papers/Can%20the%20dead%20speak.pdf

http://www.ddtdigest.com/route66/DiaryTrip2Part2.htm

http://www.desertusa.com/mag08/loretto_staircase.html

http://www.epcc.edu/nwlibrary/borderlands/17_onate_
conquered_desert.htm

http://www.epinions.com/content_170919693956

http://www.hauntsofamerica.blogspot.com/2007/12/haunting-
of-la-posada-resort.html

http://www.homepages.rootsweb. ancestry.com/~zimzip/stl/trip/
cathedral.htm

http://www.historicaltextarchive.com/sections.p?op=viewarticle
&artid=736#5

http://www.historymatters.gmu.edu/d/4929/

http://www.laposada.rockresorts.com/info/pr.13.asp

http://www.legendsofamerica.com/HC-SantaFeHauntings.html

http://www.newmexico.org/experience/museums/palace_
governors.php

http://www.newmexico.org/western/experience/grant_corner_inn.
php

http://www.newmexico.org/western/experience/julia_staab.php

http://www.newmexico.org/western/experience/la_fonda.php

http://www.newmexico.org/western/experience/la_residencia.
php

http://www.newmexicohistory.org/filedetails.php?fileID=413

http://www.rmasa.org/_wsn/page4.html

http://www.santafeghostandhistorytours.com/PHOTOS.html

http://www.sgha.net/nm/santafe/lafonda.html

http://www.sgha.net/nm/santafe/nmsp.html

http://www.sgha.net/nm/santafe/stvincent.html

http://www.traditioninaction.org/History/B_005_Onate_
   Thanksgiving.html

INDEX

Acequia Madre, 214
Analco Barrio, 5, 166

Canyon Road, 175, 176,
Casa Real, 135, 136

Dragon Room, The, 168, 169, 170,
    171

El Delirio, 143, 144, 146, 147, 148,
    152, 155, 156, 157, 159,
El Farol, 178, 179, 180, 181

Fairview Cemetery, 57, 100, 102, 103

Geronimo Restaurant, 176
Grant Avenue House, 31, 32, 36, 45,
    46, 49, 51, 52, 53, 134, 190,
    191
Guadalupe Café, The, 172, 173, 174

Hotel St. Francis, 131, 132, 141

La Fonda, 23, 24, 25, 26, 28, 29,
    182, 222
La Posada, 94, 96, 97, 98, 99, 100,
    105, 107, 111, 114
La Residencia, 135, 136, 137, 139
Loretto Chapel, The, 69, 115, 117,
    120, 121, 122, 124

New Mexico Association of Counties,
    58, 59
New Mexico State Prison, 192, 193

Old Santa Fe Trail, 59
Old Pecos Trail, 132
Oldest House, The (La Casa Vieja
    de Analco), 54, 56, 70, 80,
    81, 82, 83, 84, 85, 86, 87,
    89, 91, 92, 166

Palace of the Governors, 66, 128, 129
Pink Adobe, The, 167, 168, 169, 170,
    171, 172

San Miguel Mission, 60, 63, 66, 69,
    71, 72, 73, 81
Santa Fe Indian School, 160, 161, 162,
    163, 164
Santuario de Chimayo, 75, 76
School of Advanced Research, The
    (formerly known as the School of
    American Research), 143, 146,
    148, 149, 150, 154, 155, 158,
    159
St. Francis Cathedral, 110, 111, 112,
    129, 130

Upper Crust Pizza, 166, 167